Denise & Ross Gray

The Nature of Birds

Scientific consultants to the series: WALTER TOVELL, PhD, Director, Royal Ontario Museum; J. MURRAY SPEIRS, PhD, Department of Zoology, University of Toronto

Copyright © Natural Science of Canada Limited, 1974

ALL RIGHTS RESERVED

No part of this book may be reproduced in any form
without written permission of the publisher;
short quotations may be used for book reviews.

ISBN: 0-9196-4410-4

Natural Science of Canada Limited
58 Northline Road, Toronto, Ontario   M4B 3E5

*Publisher:*Jack McClelland
*Managing Director:*William Belt
*Editor:*Stanley Fillmore
*Assistant Editor:*Kathy Vanderlinden

CONTENTS

INTRODUCTION

This book is not intended as a guide for the identification of Canada's birds: there are already excellent books available for this purpose. Rather, it is intended to give the reader some appreciation of the richness of our bird life, some understanding of the ways our birds live, the problems they face and how they surmount them.

Canada is blessed with a rich variety of birdlife: few places outside the tropics have such diversity. A recent visitor from Europe was amazed to find that the Toronto Ornithological Club tallies between 130 and 140 species during an eight-hour period on its September field days near Pickering and from eighty to ninety species on its annual Christmas counts in the Toronto region. Even in the seemingly monotonous spruce belt of northern Ontario it is not difficult for a single observer to find seventy-five species during a June morning's jaunt.

Let us take a quick glimpse at a few of the ornithological highlights that a traveller might encounter on a cross-country trip in summer, from east to west. A ship approaching Newfoundland from Europe has had an escort of fulmars, riding on stiff wings the updraft from the ship's bow, sideslipping to one side, falling back to pick up tidbits from the ship's galley,

then effortlessly overtaking the ship again, tilting this way and that to take advantage of air currents from the wave crests. On the Grand Banks they will be joined by Leach's petrels, flitting just above the waves and looking superficially like the long-winged nighthawks that zoom over our city streets. A passing iceberg may have a group of murres as passengers. In the Gulf of St Lawrence our traveller may see gannets and kittiwakes, perhaps from the big sea bird colony at Bonaventure Island, which is a must for any bird watcher in the Maritimes. Farther in along the shore of the St Lawrence common eiders loaf among the rocks: some mothers assemble the offspring of several others and appear to have tremendous families.

My favourite spot in southern Ontario is Whitby harbour and some of the nearby marshes where such rarities as little gulls and glossy ibis may be observed. Northern Ontario is the land of many warblers: probably more species of these feathered gems and more individuals summer there than anywhere else on earth. Crossing Manitoba watch for flocks of Franklin's gulls, with their look of wide-eyed amazement, following the prairie ploughs. Try to find the big, buffy

JAMES A. KNIGHT   DONALD BALDWIN   JAMES WOODFORD   WAYNE McLAREN   ROBERT COLLINS

marbled godwits in farmyard puddles near Portage. Take a side trip up to the famous Delta marsh with its ducks, geese and pelicans and the secretive little LeConte's sparrows. The saline lakes of central Saskatchewan are noted for the avocets along their borders and the redheads and canvasbacks out on the water. A trip up to Last Mountain Lake to see the sandhill cranes coming into the fields of an evening is an unforgettable experience, as are the myriads of waterfowl on the lake itself. Before crossing into Alberta be sure to visit the Cypress hills where you may see your first really western birds mingling with some more familiar in the east. My most vivid recollection of birding in Alberta was seeing a golden eagle circling above as our train puffed its way up the valley toward Banff. Banff itself is the home of mountain bluebirds – bluest of the blue.

British Columbia is unique in its birdlife, from the Clark's nutcrackers of the high mountain treetops to the violet-green swallows and chestnut-backed chickadees of Stanley Park in Vancouver. Victoria's waterfront is the home of flotillas of beautiful little harlequin ducks. Finally, as you thread your way through the islands before reaching the open Pacific watch for the little marbled murrelets that scurry away from the approaching ship just above the waves, or look up to the pines along the shores to see the big white-headed bald eagles on lofty perches.

The photographs and writings in the chapters that follow will introduce you to the fascination of bird study, will outline the role of birds in our environment and challenge us to retain as part of our Canadian heritage the beauty of form, colour and action provided by our birds.

J. MURRAY SPEIRS

9

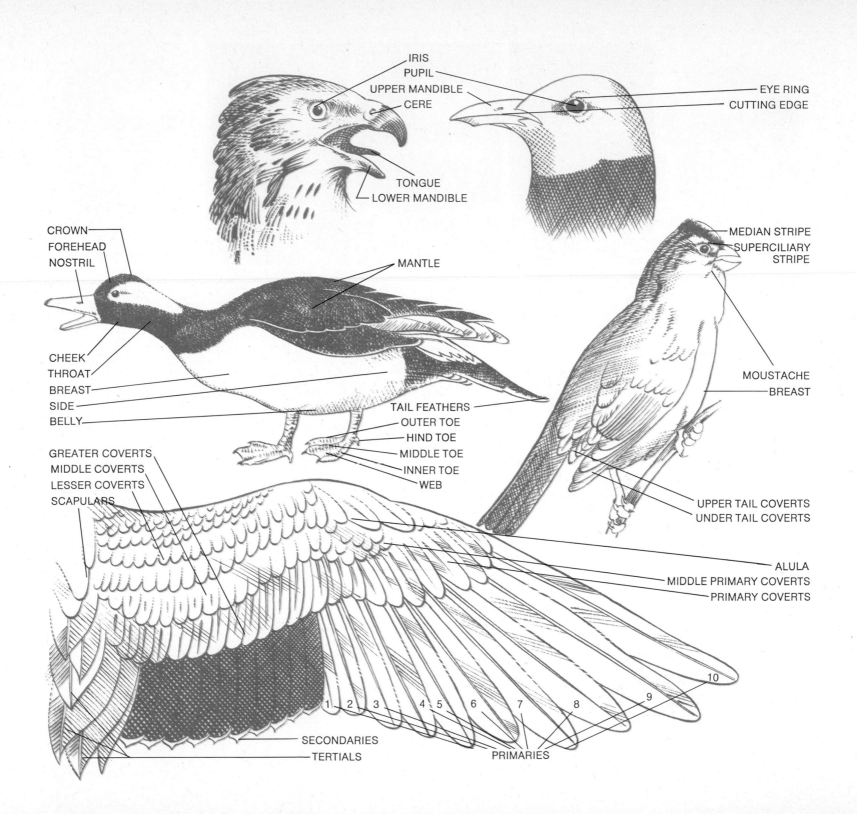

IRIS
PUPIL
UPPER MANDIBLE
CERE
TONGUE
LOWER MANDIBLE

EYE RING
CUTTING EDGE

CROWN
FOREHEAD
NOSTRIL

MANTLE

MEDIAN STRIPE
SUPERCILIARY
STRIPE

CHEEK
THROAT
BREAST
SIDE
BELLY

MOUSTACHE
BREAST

TAIL FEATHERS
OUTER TOE
HIND TOE
MIDDLE TOE
INNER TOE
WEB

GREATER COVERTS
MIDDLE COVERTS
LESSER COVERTS
SCAPULARS

UPPER TAIL COVERTS
UNDER TAIL COVERTS

ALULA
MIDDLE PRIMARY COVERTS
PRIMARY COVERTS

1 2 3 4 5 6 7 8 9 10

SECONDARIES
TERTIALS
PRIMARIES

PART ONE
WHAT IS A BIRD?

What is a bird? Anything with feathers. Other creatures fly, lay eggs, have bills, but only birds have feathers. Flight doesn't distinguish them; some birds don't even have wings, and some that do never leave the ground. There are birds that appear to hibernate, like bears. Some birds can swim as well as fish, others can burrow like moles. There are birds that fly from one end of the earth to the other – twice a year – and birds that never wander more than a few yards from the spot where they hatched. Pigeons feed their young with a product of their own bodies, but mallee fowl pay no attention whatever to their chicks.

The one thing all birds share is a covering of feathers.

Feathers are marvellous. There is nothing more stiffly strong for its weight than the flight feather of a bird, those graceful plumes at the ends of its wings that can twist and spread to control the air. At first glance they look like paddles, thin enough to transmit light. But their solidity is illusion – their structure is a web of thin barbs branching from a central shaft and connected by hairlike fibres hooked together with tiny barbs. The structure readily opens, and closes again in somewhat the same fashion as a zipper.

The bird's body is covered with feathers of this kind. Known as contour feathers, they give the bird its shape and smoothness. They're slightly oily, keep the bird dry and help water birds to float. They can be fluffed out to trap air for warmth, or pressed flat against the bird's body to conduct heat away.

But contour feathers are not the only kind birds possess. Scattered between them are hairlike feathers called filoplumes, single shafts of uncertain purpose. Many birds also possess down feathers – fluffy, rather formless tufts growing between the contour feathers. A fourth kind is possessed by a few species; known as powder-down, these feathers gradually disintegrate to dust. Herons and bitterns use the dust to dress their feathers, as mothers dust their babies with talcum.

Like the hair on our heads, feathers are dead structures. Unlike hair, feathers don't continue to grow once they are in place. They wear out, of course, in daily use and once a year (twice in some species) they are replaced. Most birds molt over an extended period, replacing feathers in pairs a few at a time so that the bird is never without the power of flight. Exceptions are the penguins, which, perhaps because they

ABOVE: *HERON* BELOW: *GULL*

ABOVE: *PUFFIN* BELOW: *BLACKBIRD*

BELOW: *COMMON FLICKER*

BELOW: *RED KNOT*

can't fly anyway, molt all at once. Ducks and geese, however, molt all their flight feathers at one time, and depend on their ability to swim to evade predators while they are flightless. The molt usually takes place in late summer, after the nesting season and in preparation for the migration or the rigours of the coming winter. Some birds molt again, partially or completely, before the nesting season in spring, perhaps in preparation for the competition of the mating season when a new coat of feathers may be an advantage in attracting a mate.

1 FEATHERS AS RADAR

Recent research by a Queen's University professor suggests that it may be the bird's feathers that give it direction on its migratory flights. Man has always speculated on how birds find their way on such flights, some of them over hundreds of miles of open water without landmarks of any kind, and often at night. Is it the sun that guides them by day and the stars by night? Is it instinct, or some form of avian radar? If it is, the receptor might be the feathers, whose sensitivity varies with temperature and humidity. A current theory holds that feathers react to the changing magnetic fields as the earth rotates, stimulating the bird to migrate along a path that reduces the stimulation. According to this theory, the feathers are so

Although superficially similar, birds of different species often display widely different characteristics. One of the noticeable differences is the feet of birds. The great blue heron has all four toes on one level, an asset in wading through shoreline waters. The yellow headed blackbird is a swamp dweller and the toes of its feet are designed to permit the bird to grasp a perch. The puffins dive for fish and their webbed feet act as powerful paddles. The black headed gull (opposite), a recent arrival in Canada, displays the webbed feet shared by all gulls. Unlike the puffin, the gulls use their webbed feet for surface swimming —not for catching fish underwater.

sensitive to temperature that they urge the migrating bird along to warmer climates as winter approaches. The theory also accounts for the confusion that causes migrating birds to lose their way over large cities, and kill themselves by flying into brightly lit buildings. The heat generated by big buildings coupled with radio waves and other electromagnetic phenomena may interfere with the natural stimuli.

The theory's major drawback is its lack of explanation of how a dead structure, the feather, can be sensitive to unseen, unheard stimuli.

Birds are not the only animals that migrate, but they are remarkable in the distance and speed of their migrations. The Arctic tern is the champion long-distance migrant of them all, flying from the Arctic to the Antarctic, a distance of 10,000 miles. Because of the long hours of daylight at the poles in summer, this bird spends more of its lifetime in the sun than any other creature.

For sheer endurance, the outstanding migrant must be the golden plover, a bird about the size of a robin. It flies from eastern Canada to South America – a distance of 2,400 miles – and arrives with a weight loss of only two ounces. That may be a great deal for a bird that weighs little more than a quarter of a pound, but it is a remarkable demonstration of the mechanical efficiency of its flight.

Powerful feet of a red tailed hawk are used to strike and carry off the bird's prey. The leather jess on the ankle identifies this bird as a captive, probably trained to hunt for small game or other birds. This hawk is one of thirteen found in Canada and breeds in every province except Newfoundland. It winters in southern US and Mexico although small numbers of the bird remain the year around in southern BC, southwestern Ontario and the Maritimes. It is seen most frequently in wooded areas but frequents open country as well; the species usually hunts in pairs. Its diet consists of snakes, frogs and smallish mammals. In recent years TV programs have suggested that training birds to hunt is a relatively easy task. As a result, hundreds–perhaps thousands–of these and other proud birds of prey have been kept in captivity only to die of neglect and abuse.

About a third of all bird species are migratory. Many birds of the northern hemisphere cross the equator on their migratory flights, but few birds that breed in the south come north. In Canada the robin is the traditional harbinger of spring, and the truth is that robins appear to migrate according to the weather, following on the heels of winter rather than advancing in spring's vanguard. The warblers come later, and usually at about the same time each year; they seem to migrate by instinct rather than weather.

In their migratory flights most birds can travel 200 to 300 miles between stops, although the rest period between flights may last for several days. Most of them fly at heights below 3,000 feet, although birds are often seen at 5,000 feet and sometimes as high as 14,000 feet – one bird was recorded by a jet pilot as flying at 20,000 feet. Their speed varies according to size and species. Small birds seldom exceed thirty miles per hour, migrating hawks may reach forty, shore birds as much as fifty, and some ducks can cruise at sixty miles per hour. In the daytime, most birds fly in great flocks, and appear to follow fairly well-defined flyways. At night, however, the flocks break up and travel singly, ranging more widely. How they find their way is still a subject of conjecture. In the case of gregarious birds it may be simply a case of follow the leader. But this cannot explain the remarkable migration of the New Zealand cuckoo; reared by non-migrating foster parents (most cuckoos lay their eggs in the nests of other birds) the young bird leaves its foster parents at the end of summer and flies 2,500 miles alone over open sea to the Solomon Islands to spend its first winter, following a track it has never seen in response to an urge of which man can only guess.

When the annual migration is accomplished, the birds set about the serious business of mating, nesting and raising young. For most of us, this renewed cycle is announced in song, usually the chirruping trill of a robin, carolling phrase after phrase from some high vantage when spring is no longer in doubt. His thrilling performance is really a challenge to other male robins in the area, defying them to enter the territory the singing male has staked out for himself. It is also a mating call and, once the birds have paired off, it is heard less and less often.

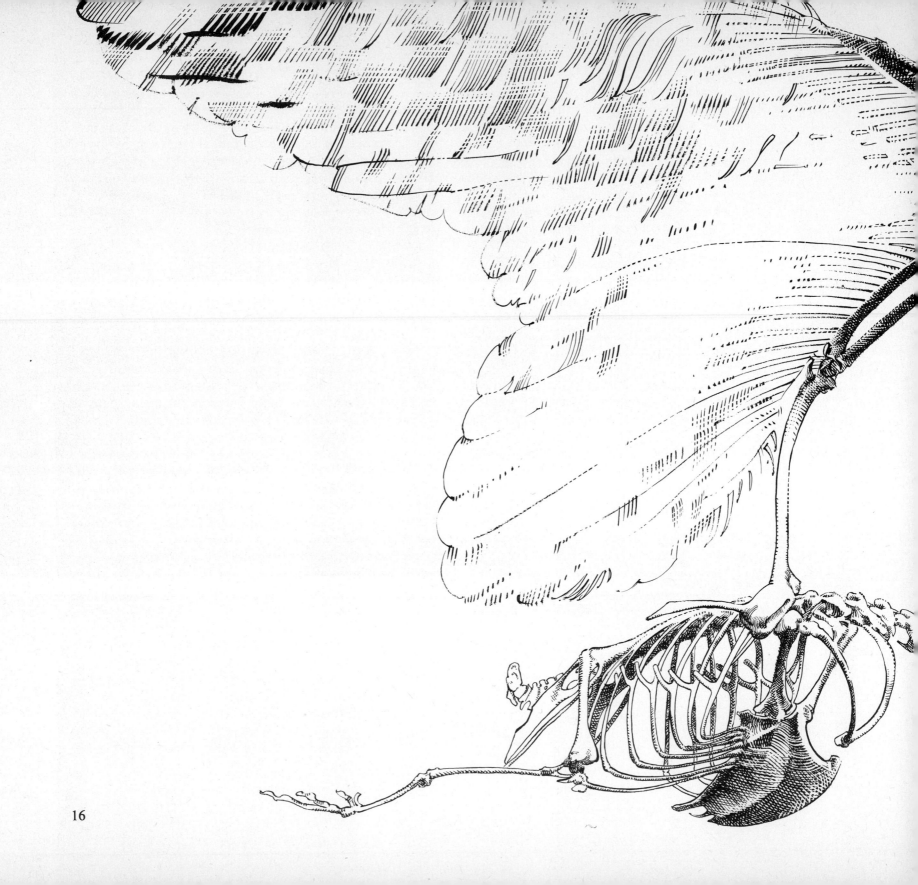

2 WANTED: ELBOW ROOM

The robin is like almost all other birds in this respect: it requires a certain amount of elbow room among its own kind. At the same time, the robin that is so quick to protect its territory against other robins has no objection to sharing the same area with any number of birds of other species. A map of robin territories would be fairly simple to draw – it would be a checkerboard, more or less, with each square covering half an acre. But a map of all the territories occupied by all the birds in an area would be a chaos of overlaps of double- and triple-occupancy.

A male bird in his own territory is virtually invincible – he has only to threaten to drive an intruding bird away. And though few birds will try to usurp a territory from a resident male, there is always a supply of bachelors available if the territorial male is caught by a cat. Indeed, the supply seems to be inexhaustible; in one experiment where the dominant male was captured and removed, a new male arrived so quickly – and so frequently – that the researchers had to abandon the experiment.

Not all birds sing to establish their territory. Some species stamp their feet, others click, snap or rattle their bills, still others rustle and clack their feathers, beat the air with their wings or drum on trees. All of their utterances are characteristic of their kind – a bird is as identifiable by its song as it is by its shape, size and colour. Furthermore, each individual bird sings in its own way, in a voice and style that can be recognized.

Of course, birds do not stop singing when the eggs are laid and the young are hatching. The territorial song may be

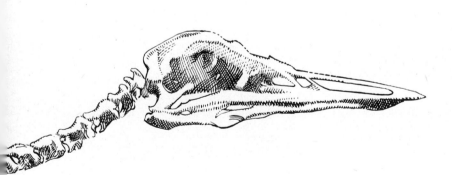

Millions of years of evolution have modified the skeleton of birds for life on the wing. The bones are frequently hollow, a great saving in weight. The deep sternum is the bone to which the powerful wing muscles are attached. The most striking adaptation is the modification of the forelimbs into wings.

heard less frequently, but birds use their voices for other purposes as well. The oilbird of South America spends its days sleeping so deep in caves that it uses a form of sonar to find its way out, emitting a clicking sound and navigating by the echoes that bounce back from the cave walls.

Birds also sing at evening, which many people find pleasantly plaintive, and this song may be emotional, in the sense that a dog baying at the moon is vocalizing without any obvious practical purpose. Birds also use their voices to announce the presence of a food source to other birds of its kind, to keep in touch with other members of a flock, to call their young, or to warn of danger. The raucous call of a jay warns every forest creature that something unusual is afoot, and the hysterical shrieking of robins when their young are learning to fly calls every bird in the neighbourhood to join the frantic parents.

For robins, this harrowing experience takes place twice a summer since, like many Canadian birds, they raise two broods a season, each of three or four young. Like most land birds, they can begin breeding the first year and continue to raise young throughout a life span of about four years. Other birds are even more fecund – the female rhea, an ostrich-like bird of South America, lays as many as sixty eggs to a clutch and then departs; the male incubates them. A dozen eggs are common in the nests of many ducks and pheasants, and their total mass is often greater than the mother's. The ruddy duck, which weighs half a pound, lays an average of eight or nine eggs to a clutch, weighing a total of about two pounds – four times the mother's weight. This fantastic rate of replacement permits an enormous annual duck harvest without any appreciable effect on duck populations; individuals shot by hunters in the fall are replaced the next spring.

But other birds are less fruitful. The albatross, which spends its life sailing the air currents of the seven seas on its eleven-foot wings – it can relax as completely in the air as a fish can in water, so exquisitely is it adapted to the wind – does not begin to breed before it is nine years old, and then it lays only one egg. But an albatross has few enemies, and one egg at a time is enough to maintain the species's population.

3 HELPLESS HATCHLINGS

When a young bird hatches from the egg after an incubation period that may be as short as eleven days or as long as eighty, depending on the species, it may be at any stage of maturity ranging from virtual helplessness to self-sufficiency. The young of the warblers which constitute the greatest number of birds in Canadian forests can do little more than raise their heads and gape for food when they hatch. Their industrious parents stuff them with insects, and they grow at a tremendous rate; in a few days they can leave the nest, although they still depend on the parents for food. Young sandpipers and pheasants can run after their parents as soon as they are dry after hatching, and young ducks can swim. The chicks of the mallee fowl of southeast Asia are the most advanced of all birds at hatching – they can fly as soon as their feathers are dry, and they must look after themselves from the beginning, for the parents take no interest in them.

The 'nest' of the mallee fowl, if it can be called that, is one of the strangest made by birds – a heap of earth scratched up by the male around a core of leaves, sticks and other vegetable matter. The female lays her eggs in this compost pile and the male attends them, piling on more earth to raise the incubation temperature as the decaying compost generates heat, or scratching it away if the temperature gets too high. It takes at least two months for a mallee egg to hatch and, since the eggs are laid over a period of months, the male mallee fowl has virtually a lifetime job looking after his mound nest.

Some birds have no use for a nest of any kind; nighthawks lay their eggs directly on the gravel roofs of downtown buildings, and some sea birds lay on bare ledges on the cliffs of sea islands. In such circumstances, the egg's only protection is its

An x-ray of an American kestrel, formerly called a sparrow hawk, clearly shows the thin, narrow strips of bones called the uncinate processes, which reinforce the bird's rib cage.

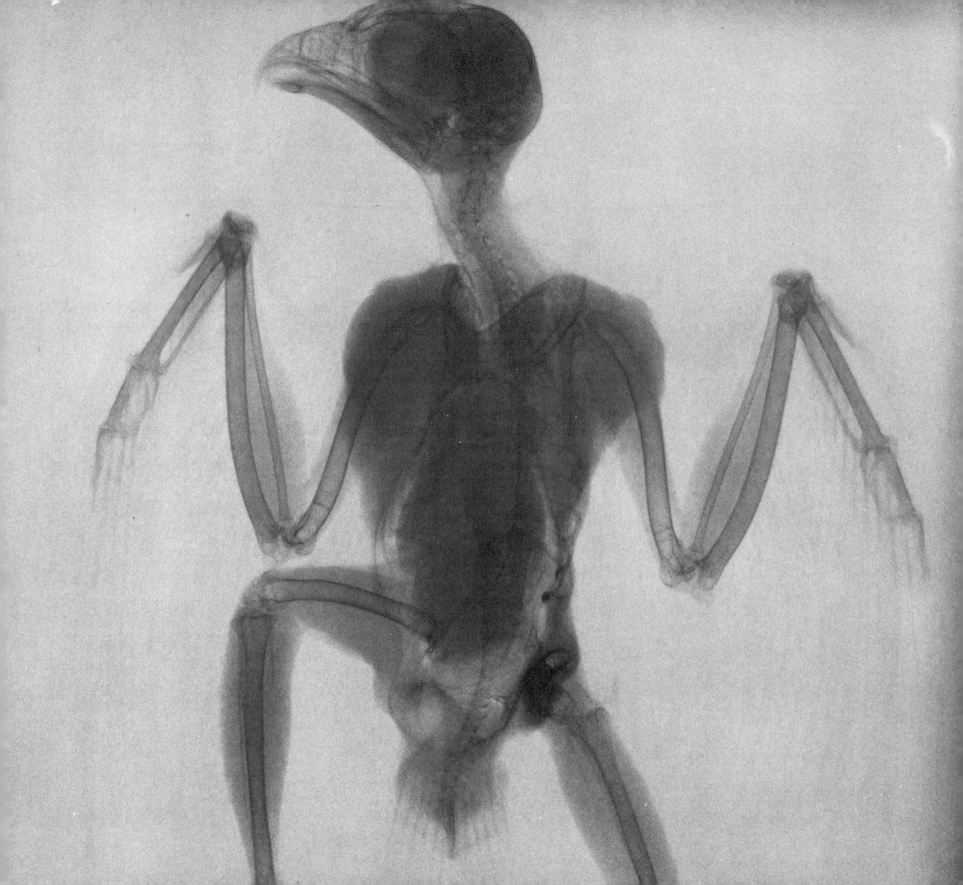

ABOVE: *FLICKER* BELOW: *HERRING GULL* | ABOVE: *KINGFISHER* BELOW: *SANDPIPER* | ABOVE: *NUTCRACKER* BELOW: *SWIFT* | ABOVE: *WILD TURKEY* BELOW: *CUCKOO*

BELOW: *WHISTLING SWAN* | BELOW: *GANNET* | BELOW: *BLACK SKIMMER* | BELOW: *WHITE PELICAN*

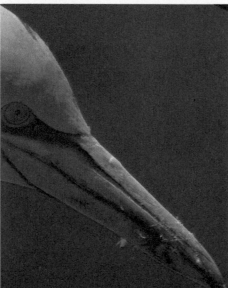

ABOVE: *PUFFIN* BELOW: *TURKEY VULTURE*   ABOVE: *BARRED OWL* BELOW: *GOSHAWK*

BELOW: *RING-NECKED PHEASANT*   BELOW: *LESSER YELLOWLEGS*

shape – sharply pointed at one end, it rolls in a tight circle, with less danger of falling off. Between these two extremes lie nests of almost every conceivable kind – tunnels bored in the face of sand and clay cliffs or in the wood of trees, floating rafts used by grebes, the robin's grass-lined mud cup, the elegant purses woven by orioles to swing on the tips of tree branches, the tiny moss-and-cobweb thimbles of the hummingbirds, the sturdy mortar bowls glued by swallows under the eaves of barns, the awkward sticks-and-leaves contraptions of crows, and the untidy heaps of straw thrown together by sparrows. The ovenbirds of South America build football-sized nests, as hard as concrete, on top of fence posts and telephone poles. The cave swifts of the far east build nests of their own saliva, which hardens like glue on exposure to air; it is these nests that are used to make the famous Chinese delicacy, bird's nest soup.

Of course, there are birds that neither build nests nor care for their young – parasites that lay their eggs in the nests of other birds who then raise these foster-young, often to the detriment of their own offspring. The cowbird is the most notorious example in Canada; the female often lays her egg in the nest of a much smaller bird, and when the cowbird hatches it is bigger and grows faster than the other nestlings, often starving them to death since the cowbird's size and strength keep it in the forefront at feeding time. The hustling parents simply stuff the food into the most prominently gaping mouth – the cowbird's. The interloper usually soon outgrows the parents, and after leaving the cramped nest still relies on them for food. Apparently proud of their gigantic 'offspring' the diminutive parents oblige until the cowbird

The shape and size of a bird's beak is a clue to its eating habits. Long, slender bills are associated with probers – birds that stick their bills into trees or water to dislodge insects, crustaceans and worms. A hooked bill like that worn by the goshawk identifies a bird of prey; the hooked upper mandible is used for tearing flesh. Short, stubby bills identify seed and nut eaters. The pouch under the pelican's bill is used as a seine to scoop up quantities of fish. In the words of the old nursery rhyme: 'A peculiar bird is the pelican/Whose beak can hold more than its belly can.'

21

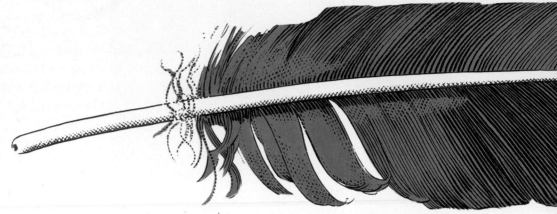

can fend for itself. Some eighty species of birds are entirely parasitic, but some are partly parasitic, building their own nests but also laying eggs in the nests of other birds. The cuckoo's habit of laying eggs in the nests of other birds has given a word to our language: to be a cuckold is to have the nest of your marriage invaded by an outsider.

But if cuckold is an apt expression, the phrase 'eating like a bird' to describe a person who picks at his food, is not. Birds are voracious eaters – a young warbler will consume its own weight in insects every day. Adult birds that feed on insects must consume about forty percent of their own weight in bugs every day; seed-eaters consume about ten percent, due to the smaller percentage of water in seeds. The activity that demands such enormous amounts of food is prodigious. If a 170-pound man expended energy at the rate of a hummingbird, it has been calculated that he would have to perspire one hundred pounds of water every hour to keep his skin from boiling. He would also have to eat double his own weight in potatoes every day, or one-and-one-half times his weight in meat. Of course, the hummingbird lives at a rate faster than any other bird – its wings beat fifty to seventy times per second; a pigeon beats its wings only five to eight times per second. Actually, the hummingbird achieves its hovering flight by moving its wings in a kind of circular motion rather than flapping them as other birds do.

4 VORACIOUS FEEDERS

Such frenetic activity requires constant replenishment of food. The appetite that permits birds to live at such high metabolic rates is at times a blessing to man and at other times a curse. The voracity of birds keeps insect populations at tolerable levels, and can be a factor where crops are threatened by insects. But the reverse is also true, as anyone whose cherry tree has been stripped by robins can attest. In fact, there is scarcely anything edible that birds won't eat, and some birds thrive on diets that are poisonous to man. Vultures, for example, feed on carrion, apparently unaffected by the products of putrefaction that produce ptomaine poisoning. There are birds that can eat wax – they harbour a bacteria that can digest this substance. Birds eat fish, flesh and other fowl. They live on nectar, flowers, fruit, seeds, leaves and branches of plants. Woodpeckers shoot their barbed tongues deep into insect holes to catch wood-boring grubs. Night-hawks catch mosquitoes on the wing – several thousand flying insects of more than fifty species were counted in one bird's stomach. Flickers eat ants, oblivious to the acidic secretions that make other birds avoid them – one investigator

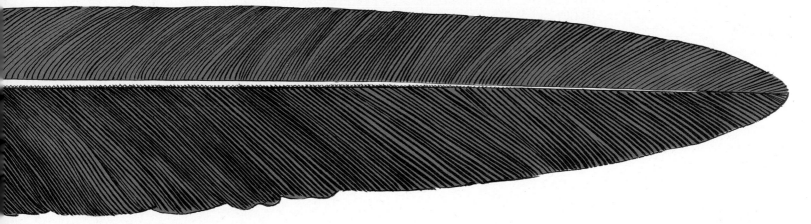

counted 5,040 ants in a flicker's stomach. Flamingos strain the mud of shallow ponds for tiny water creatures, loons dive for fish (unlike most birds, they have solid bones, an advantage under water), and scoters eat clams and oysters, shells and all. Strangest of all are the grebes that stuff their stomachs with feathers torn from their own bodies after each meal. Why? No one really knows.

Although some birds will eat virtually anything, most birds tend to follow a fairly limited diet, feeding on the same things year after year. Accordingly, their numbers tend to fluctuate with their food supply, rising after good years, and declining after lean ones. The northern shrike population follows the four-year cycle of the mouse-like voles on which it preys, building up as the food supply increases, then crashing when the voles disappear. But birds are mobile creatures, and most of them are adaptable to changed circumstances. They can leave their accustomed haunts when the food supply diminishes, and range far afield in search of food. When this happens they are seen in parts of the country where they are usually unknown; the snowy owl of the Arctic ranges as far south as the Great Lakes in search of food when the lemmings disappear. Sometimes storms blow migrating birds off course, carrying them to new lands that can be to their liking. This happened to a colony of African cattle egrets, which showed up in British Guiana in the 1930s and found the new world so much to their liking that they had spread north to Canada by 1962 and are now seen in all provinces from Manitoba east.

Many birds are as genetically malleable as the egrets are geographically adaptable. The canary is a case in point. In the wild, it is rather drab, streaked olive-brown above and yellowish below, with no voice to speak of. Selective breeding has produced from this unpromising little finch the epitome of the songbird, a creature with an unmatched repertoire that can warble and trill the day long, resplendent in a dazzling coat that ranges from deep orange, through brilliant yellow to pure white. Perhaps even more astonishing is the variety of domestic chickens that have been bred from a common ancestor – the jungle fowl of southeast Asia. The new world's contribution is the barnyard turkey, a development of the wild turkey of North America.

Like all living creatures, birds are links in the evolutionary chain that stretches back to the mysterious beginnings of life and points forward to unimaginable mutations yet to come. The ostrich is an example: although it's a bird, it's a very large creature – some of them weigh 300 pounds. Long ago, ostriches lost the power of flight, and have evolved as grazing animals of the plains. Like most grazing animals, they have only two toes (other birds have four, usually), and it has been suggested that the ostrich is on the way to developing a single toe, like the horse.

23

5 REPTILIAN ANCESTORS

The ancestors of birds are considered to have been reptiles, and birds still share with reptiles the scales on their legs and feet and the fact that they lay eggs. They also share another characteristic – a third eye in the top of the head. Known as the pineal eye, this organ is found in some fishes and reptiles and in embryo birds. It has disappeared by the time the bird hatches, however, and even among fishes and reptiles, its function is in doubt.

Generally speaking, the eyes of birds are the most acute in nature. For the size of the creature, they are huge, usually larger than the brain, although not much shows on the outside. The enormous eyeballs rest immovable in bony sockets that constitute most of the skull. The nocturnal Australian frogmouth has eyes so large that they project into the roof of the bird's big mouth and are visible there through the thin bony covering. It was thought that the frogmouth looked out through its gaping mouth to sight on the flying insects it catches on the wing.

The extraordinary acuteness of bird's eyesight is due to three things: a retina densely packed with vision cells; an area in the eye so constructed that it acts to magnify images falling on it; and an arrangement of muscles that manipulate the lens to focus sharply on an insect egg as close as an inch from a bird's beak, or a hawk flying several hundred feet above. The placing of the eyes at the sides of the head also gives most birds a very great field of vision – they can see objects on both sides of them at once, as well as in front. The woodcock's eyes are placed so that it can actually see behind it, to both sides and in front, all at the same time. An exception is the owl, whose eyes are placed in the front of its head, like man's. Owls see only in front of them, in three dimensions: to see behind they must turn their heads completely around on their flexible necks, since the eyes are all but fixed in their sockets.

In addition to the embryonic third eye, birds also have three eyelids; a top and bottom lid on each eye that meet in the mid-

Flight, the most distinctive behaviour pattern of birds, is illustrated in the direct line flight of the whistling swans (opposite) *and the hovering flight of the hummingbird* (above). *The whistlers breed in the muskeg of Canada's north and migrate to winter homes in California and the Atlantic seaboard of the* US.

dle when they close, and a third membrane that varies from translucent to transparent and sweeps across the eye to clean and moisten the cornea. In hawks especially, this transparency permits the bird to maintain its scrutiny of the ground below for the tiny movements that betray its prey while keeping its eyes clean and lubricated.

The marvellous adaptations that have made it possible for birds to establish themselves in every corner of the globe except for the interior of Antarctica have sometimes backfired. The great auk is a case in point. A flightless sea bird with few natural enemies, it lived in the North Atlantic, breeding securely on rocky islands off Newfoundland. But when men began sailing those seas, the great auk afforded easily obtained provisions, and was ruthlessly hunted. The stubby wings that made it so efficient at sea rendered it unable to escape the hungry sailors on land and the last pair were killed in Iceland in 1844. The penguins of the Antarctic are beautifully adapted to their life on the edge of the south polar seas, but this could be their undoing – any change is likely to be the worse for them.

It isn't that way with all birds, however, even where man moves in to create wholesale changes in the countryside by levelling forests, planting farms, building cities. For every bird that is displaced by these activities, another finds the changes to its liking. Cutting the forest may displace the woodpecker, but the farm attracts the meadowlark. Even the cities provide acceptable habitats for birds, and not only for the starlings, pigeons and sparrows that are so common. Swifts, nighthawks and martins commonly nest on tall buildings, and sift the city skies for insects. Even the peregrine falcon, the wildest of the hawks, has been known to nest on the ledges of skyscrapers.

---

6 A NICHE FOR EVERY BIRD

Indeed, every place where man settles provides a niche for some bird. The pigeon has made the centre of the city his own, sharing the handouts of office workers with sparrows and starlings. The suburbs, with their cultivated gardens and yards, are home to robins, wrens, chipping sparrows, warblers, song sparrows, orioles, cardinals, blue jays and crows. Along the roadside live kingbirds, shrikes, song sparrows and bluebirds. Phoebes and swallows nest on the rafters of barns, and owls hunt mice in their dusty interiors. Cliff swallows nest under the eaves of barns, cowbirds follow the cattle in the fields to scoop up the insects they disturb, and pheasants mingle with the chickens in the barnyard. The orchard is home to wrens, titmice, woodpeckers, flycatchers, goldfinches, robins, waxwings and screech owls. Bird houses in the trees attract bluebirds, swallows and wrens, and whole colonies of purple martins know no other homes than the compartmented boxes raised for them in clearings.

Wherever man goes, and whatever he does, a host of birds follow to exploit the opportunities he creates for them.

In Canada and some other countries of the world birds are provided some legal protection, and the dangers that face them are recognized. Species that are near extinction are treated with great care – the annual migration of the whooping crane from its nesting area in Wood Buffalo Park in the Northwest Territories to its wintering area on the Texas coast of the Gulf of Mexico is a time of great anxiety for bird-lovers in Canada and the United States. North Americans were not always so careful, and the extinction of the passenger pigeon is a sad example of the results of unthinking action. Once so numerous that its flocks actually darkened the sky, and trees collapsed under the weight of birds roosting on their branches, this species was killed off entirely – the last bird died in a Cincinnati zoo in 1914. Part of the reason for the passenger pigeon's extinction lay in its reproduction pattern – it laid only one egg a year, and this low reproduction rate was unable to offset the annual losses through hunting and natural predation. Eventually there were not enough birds to maintain the species, and it disappeared. The reason the same thing is unlikely with ducks, which are intensively hunted, lies in the large number of eggs they lay every season which guarantees a large number of new individuals every year. This fecundity permitted the greater snow goose to recover from the threat of extinction it faced in the 1900s when the species was down to an estimated 3,000 birds. The observance of strict conservation measures, particularly bag limits at the hunting preserves of Cap Tourmente in Quebec where the flock traditionally stops on its migration from the Arctic, has increased the population to an estimated 125,000 birds. In many countries, however, there is no protection for birds, and they are shot, trapped, netted or poisoned for a wide variety of reasons – food, sport, protection of crops. The peregrine falcon, an endangered species that nests in the

---

A flight of Canada geese in the familiar V-formation heads north on its spring migration.
Overleaf: *The gyrfalcon of the high Arctic surveys its domain. Like all falcons this species has a toothed upper mandible.*

Northwest Territories, faces an unusual hazard – it is the most highly prized bird among falconers, and where this sport is practised, particularly in the middle east, a healthy, wild peregrine falcon can be sold for as much as $30,000. With that kind of a price on its head, the falcons are hunted by poachers who balance the risk of being caught against the possible profits.

There is an absolute ban on the taking of peregrine falcons, but open seasons are permitted for the shooting of birds of other species. The greater snow geese, which were nearly exterminated seventy years ago, are 'harvested' each fall by hunters chosen in a sort of lottery. In 1972, 448 hunters bagged 526 geese, and it has been estimated they paid $93.62 each for them. All told, the sport hunting of birds in Canada is a multi-million dollar business; in 1961, the last year for which figures are available, Canadians spent more than $27 million on hunting. The figure is probably higher today but with accurate management, it's a business that should last forever, with this year's hatch providing birds for next fall's harvest.

Of even greater economic importance to Canada are domestic fowl – chickens, turkeys, ducks and geese. Chickens are by far the most prominent – there are about three and one-half chickens for every person in Canada, and their value as meat is close to $200 million. If you add all the chickens, turkeys, ducks and geese together you get a population of close to eighty million, and a value close to $275 million.

The life of a domestic bird raised for the table is restricted in the extreme. Most of them are raised in huge chicken factories, where the bird exists in cages throughout its development, never seeing the light of day, fed controlled amounts of food and water, doctored with chemicals, illuminated and darkened on schedule, and killed and marketed to meet a timetable. In contrast, the wild bird, even with all the hazards it faces in life, is indeed free. And it may reach a ripe old age, for a bird. There is a case on record of an oystercatcher that was banded as a chick in 1929; the band was recovered from the bird in 1959 – thirty years later. Other birds may live longer in captivity – claims for parrots with ages greater than one hundred years are sometimes heard – but only a leg band can verify the age of a wild bird.

A great blue heron (opposite) *launches itself from a treetop. Largest of twelve Canadian species the great blue is often mistaken for a sandhill crane of the Prairies. The sandhill flies with neck extended; the great blue with neck folded back. The Canada goose* (above) *honks madly on take off.*

The systematic banding of birds has been going on for nearly a century, although the practice goes back even further to 1740 when a German tied coloured string to the legs of swallows. Today, more than half a million birds are banded every year in North America by dedicated bird-watchers and wildlife service officers. Throughout the world the total number banded is well more than ten million, and returned bands provide information about bird migrations, ages, locations, and the rise and fall of populations. They even tell something about speed, for a yellowlegs banded on Cape Cod was caught six days later in Martinique – 1,900 miles away.

JAMES A. KNIGHT

31

PART TWO
THE SHAPING HAND
OF EVOLUTION

One hundred and forty million years ago in central Europe, a crow-sized animal took off from its tree perch and flew. Its flight was in the nature of a shallow glide, for its ability to flap its wings was poor. Offshore winds carried it out over water. Perhaps a sudden gust of wind or reaching wave-top was its undoing, for it ended up on the bottom of a large but shallow tropical lake and was subsequently buried in soft sediments which, in time, hardened into limestone. The animal's bones and incontestable evidence of feathers became fossilized. When the fossils came to light in the 1860s they provided science with direct evidence of the origin of birds from a period much earlier than hitherto thought – from the age of reptiles.

We are extremely fortunate to have these early fossils, for birds are not ideally designed for fossilization, as were the mighty dinosaurs, and the precise conditions conducive to

Wild turkey, now almost completely vanished from south-western Ontario, is an ancestor of the barnyard fowl. Seven species are known, each from North American deposits.

fossil formation are rarely met with. Birds are, in the main, too small and their hollow, fragile bones too light to survive predators, scavengers and the process of decay. The story of the origin, and early evolution of birds is therefore sketchy, and dependent upon fragmentary evidence. When fossilized bird bones are found, they are typically the remains of only the heavier portions of the larger bones, and the bias is always towards water birds – sedimentary deposits have always been amongst the best preservatives. The earliest known fossil 'bird' represented by three more or less complete specimens and a single feather, were all found within ten miles of each other in Bavaria, in slate quarries famous for their fine textured limestones, used in the manufacture of lithographic printing plates.

The first discovery in 1860, tantalizing and dramatic, was of a single contour feather which came to light with the striking of a quarryman's hammer upon virgin limestone. Thus was discovered the earliest evidence of the presence on earth of birds 140 million years ago. It was not much, but its implications were great. It focussed the attentions of the small, scattered paleontological community upon the site

FAMILY ANATIDAE
SWANS, GEESE AND DUCKS
of North America

Based on the American Ornithologists' Union Checklist, fifth edition, 1957 and Delacour's *Waterfowl of the World*, 1959.

SUBFAMILY (1)

Cygninae
SWANS

MUTE SWAN
Cygnus olor

WHISTLING SWAN
Olor columbianus

TRUMPETER SWAN
Olor buccinator

SUBFAMILY (2)

Anserinae
GEESE

CANADA GOOSE
Branta canadensis
B.c. canadensis
B.c. interior
B.c. maxima
B.c. moffitti
B.c. parvipes
B.c. fulva
B.c. occidentalis
B.c. leucopareia
B.c. hutchinsii
B.c. minima

BRANT
Branta bernicla hrota

BLACK BRANT
Branta nigricans

EMPEROR GOOSE
Philacte canagica

WHITE-FRONTED GOOSE
Anser albifrons
A.a. frontalis
A.a. gambelli

SNOW GOOSE
Chen caerulescens
C.c. caerulescens
C.c. atlantica

ROSS'S GOOSE
Chen rossii

SUBFAMILY (3)

Dendrocygninae
TREE DUCKS

BLACK-BELLIED TREE DUCK
Dendrocygna autumnalis fulgens

FULVOUS TREE DUCK
Dendrocygna bicolor helva

SUBFAMILY (4)

Anatinae
SURFACE-FEEDING DUCKS

MALLARD
Anas platyrhynchos platyrhynchos

MEXICAN DUCK
Anas diazi novimexicana

BLACK DUCK
Anas rubripes

MOTTLED DUCK
Anas fulvigula
A.f. fulvigula
A.f. maculosa

GADWALL
Anas strepera

PINTAIL
Anas acuta

GREEN-WINGED TEAL
Anas crecca
A.c. crecca
A.c. carolinensis

BLUE-WINGED TEAL
Anas discors
A.d. discors
A.d. orphna

CINNAMON TEAL
Anas cyanoptera septentrionalium

EUROPEAN WIGEON
Anas penelope

AMERICAN WIGEON
Anas americana

SHOVELLER
Anas clypeata

WOOD DUCK
Aix sponsa

SUBFAMILY (5)

Aythyinae
DIVING DUCKS

REDHEAD
Aythya americana

RING-NECKED DUCK
Aythya collaris

CANVASBACK
Aythya valisineria

GREATER SCAUP
Aythya marila nearctica

LESSER SCAUP
Aythya affinis

COMMON GOLDENEYE
Bucephala clangula americana

BARROW'S GOLDENEYE
Bucephala islandica

BUFFLEHEAD
Bucephala albeola

OLDSQUAW
Clangula hyemalis

HARLEQUIN DUCK
Histrionicus histrionicus

STELLER'S EIDER
Polysticta stelleri

COMMON EIDER
Somateria mollisima
S.m. borealis
S.m. dresseri
S.m. sedentaria
S.m.v – nigra

KING EIDER
Somateria spectabilis

SPECTACLED EIDER
Somateria fischeri

BLACK SCOTER
Melanitta nigra

WHITE-WINGED SCOTER
Melanitta deglandi
M.d. deglandi
M.d. dixoni

SURF SCOTER
Melanitta perspicillata

SUBFAMILY (6)

Oxyurinae
RUDDY & MASKED DUCKS

RUDDY DUCK
Oxyura jamaicensis rubida

SUBFAMILY (7)

Merginae
MERGANSERS

HOODED MERGANSER
Lophodytes cucullatus

COMMON MERGANSER
Mergus merganser americanus

RED-BREASTED MERGANSER
Mergus serrator serrator

THIS CLASSIFICATION CHART SHOWS THE 46 SPECIES OF *ANATIDAE* THAT OCCUR REGULARLY IN NORTH AMERICA.

near Solnhofen. Scientists visited, more tangible evidence was sought, and rewards were offered. One year later, an almost complete skeleton was found. Like its predecessor it passed first to the fossil-collecting medical officer of the district of Pappenheim, who often received specimens from the quarrymen in exchange for his medical services. It might easily have been taken for that of a small dinosaur, except that the fossil included the tell-tale impression of feathers. It was named *Archaeopteryx lithographica* (now in the British Museum). The generic name *Archaeopteryx* means 'ancient wing,' the specific name *lithographica* honours the limestone deposit which preserved it.

The second skeletal specimen (also in the British Museum) was uncovered in 1877 and was at first named *Archaeopteryx seimensi*. The third, a partial skeleton (now in the University of Erlangen) was found in 1958 in the same quarry as the first skeleton but twenty feet below the first level. However, in 1954, Sir Gavin de Beer, after a detailed analysis of the two earlier specimens, concluded that both were in fact of the same species. Such minute differences as existed could easily be accounted for by variations due to age and sex. Today, the reptilian origin of birds is widely accepted and fairly obvious even to the layman, considering the reptilian scales still retained on the feet and legs of modern birds. There are similarities too, in egg-laying and embryology. What the Victorian scientists were confronted with was a perfect 'missing link,' an animal clearly transitional between true reptile and true bird. For a while there was heated argument as to what classification *Archaeopteryx* should receive. Paleontologists finding clear evidence of avian affinities – particularly the feathers – argued for its recognition as a bird. As recently as 1944 it was suggested that *Archaeopteryx* was a tree-climbing dinosaur, which should take its place at the top of the reptilian scale rather than at the bottom of the avian. Now we see these arguments merely as evidence of the difficulty with which man imposes his own artificial system of classification upon the dynamic ongoing forces of living and evolving organisms.

The reptilian characteristics of *Archaeopteryx* most closely resemble those of the *Pseudosuchia*, a group of small extinct thecodent (socket-toothed) reptiles which existed in the old world during the earlier half of the Triassic period. To seek out the true evolution of modern birds, therefore, one must go back fully 200 million years. We may never know just which of those small, agile, early dinosaurs gave rise to *Archaeopteryx*.

7 FEATHERS FROM SCALES

That *Archaeopteryx* should be clearly part reptile and part bird reassures us in the modern theory of the avian descent from reptiles. Around the established fact of *Archaeopteryx* and the level of avian progress it represented can be hung all manner of recent evidence to enlighten and support our knowledge of this monumental evolutionary process. Modern chemical analysts have compared the chemistry of a single reptilian scale with that of a bird's feather and found a remarkable similarity. Even the periodic shedding of a reptile's scales is mirrored in the seasonal molting of a bird's feathers.

Like the earlier thecodents *Archaeopteryx* was a carnivore, perhaps in part insectivorous, whose teeth were needed to grasp its prey. From climbing in search of food and to escape ground predators, it was a logical development to squirrel-like jumps between trees and the ability ultimately to glide. We know now that it is behaviour which dictates the anatomy. The bird has acquired his wings as the end result of all his early attempts at flight. Similar examples are found amongst modern reptiles, amphibians, and mammals. But where these animals have developed webs of skin between fore and hind limbs to support their gliding activities, *Archaeopteryx* went one better. It evolved from the reptilian scale that marvel of lightness, strength and adaptability, the feather. True flight comes with the ability to take off and rise under one's own power, to go upwards as well as forward, and this *Archaeopteryx* couldn't do. Its sternum was too small, there were no large breast muscles to enable it to flap strongly upwards. It had at best the ability to soar on updrafts and to extend its glide with feeble wing movements. Its long tail was clearly

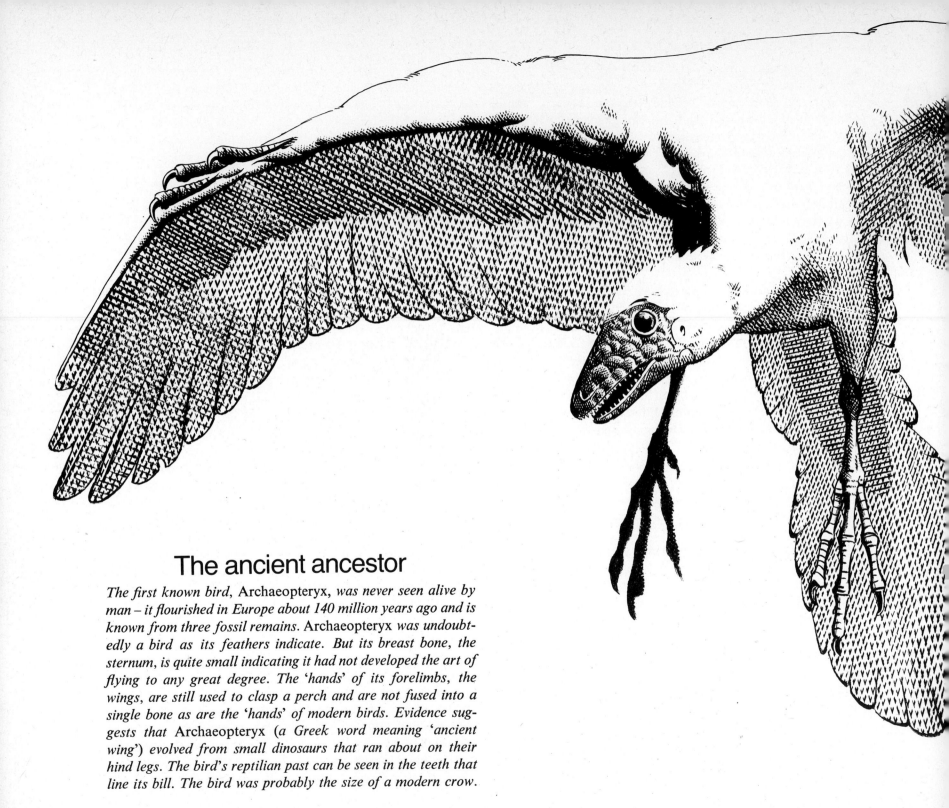

The ancient ancestor

The first known bird, Archaeopteryx, was never seen alive by man – it flourished in Europe about 140 million years ago and is known from three fossil remains. Archaeopteryx was undoubtedly a bird as its feathers indicate. But its breast bone, the sternum, is quite small indicating it had not developed the art of flying to any great degree. The 'hands' of its forelimbs, the wings, are still used to clasp a perch and are not fused into a single bone as are the 'hands' of modern birds. Evidence suggests that Archaeopteryx (a Greek word meaning 'ancient wing') evolved from small dinosaurs that ran about on their hind legs. The bird's reptilian past can be seen in the teeth that line its bill. The bird was probably the size of a modern crow.

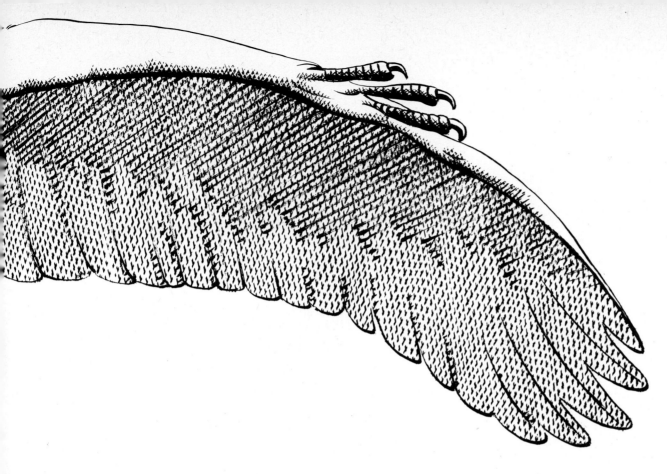

reptilian, composed of numerous vertebrae, but growing out of the tail were feathers.

Its toes and claws were well developed for grasping and climbing. At the wrist of the wing, articulating with the metacarpals were three separate fingers (the middle one longest) each becoming a long, curved, sharply pointed claw. It was therefore well equipped for an arboreal existence.

The single 140 million-year-old feather, eleven millimetres wide and sixty-eight long, found in 1860 was already as complete and perfect as that of any modern bird. It gives no hint of what must have been a very long evolutionary progression from the reptilian scale. Doubtless *Archaeopteryx* had its partially feathered ancestors. Several are the theories to explain how the evolution may have come to pass. We must also ask ourselves – why? Birds did not pioneer flight. When *Archaeopteryx* and its progenitors lived their arboreal lives in that lush, tropical landscape, winged dinosaurs, all doomed to extinction, already flew overhead on leathery wings. Mil-

lions of years before them, insects, many of them giant by modern standards, flew far and wide. What then was the secret of the early birds' success? Again the answer is undoubtedly the feather. Between *Archaeopteryx* and the modern birds, the feather has evolved as nature's most perfect means of flight – pinions and tail feathers for propulsion and manoeuvering, body feathers for streamlining and insulation. We do not know at what stage birds became homeothermic (warm-blooded) – some evidence suggests *Archaeopteryx* may have begun the process – but in time they did achieve it, and whereas the coming of colder climates contributed to, or caused, the decline of the dinosaurs, birds now had efficient feather insulation to retain body heat and adapt to the widening range of temperatures. Equipped with feathers, hollow bones, and, in time, larger than reptilian brains, the birds, after sharing the skies with the pterosaurs for one hundred million years, truly conquered the air and were poised to colonize the earth.

37

ICHTHYORNIS

HESPERORNIS

Ichthyornis, *a word meaning 'fish bird' was a gull-like creature that flourished about eighty-five million years ago. Its well developed sternum indicates it was a powerful flier. Sea birds were more likely than land birds to be fossilized on the shores of the vast oceans which covered much of the world during the Cretaceous period.*

Hesperornis (*western bird*), *a flightless diving bird about six feet long, was found in North America. At one time flightless birds were thought to represent a stage in evolution before birds learned to fly. Now, flightless birds are considered to have given up flying; some, like the penguin, merely substitute water for air as the medium in which to fly.*

PHORORHACOS

DIATRYMA

Phororhacos, *a five-foot-tall bird of Brazil and Argentina, lived some twenty to forty million years ago. Its powerful legs indicate that the bird was a good runner and its enormous curved beak – like the bills of today's eagles and hawks – identify it as a carnivore.* Phororhacos *is one of about 900 species of birds identified from fossils.*

Diatryma, *a fearsome predator of the Tertiary period about sixty million years ago, has been studied in fossil forms found in North America and Central Europe. Standing nearly seven feet high, the bird was an antecedent of today's cranes. Its bulky body was topped with a short neck, a large head and a vicious bill.*

8 NATURE ABHORS A VACUUM

Nature abhors a vacuum. The evolutionary process of life has always moved to fill all the space available for it and birds were destined to cover the globe more completely than any earlier vertebrate group. Oceans and deserts could be crossed, mountain ranges surmounted or flown around. In order to realize their biological potential they would evolve countless forms of infinite variety.

The fossil record shows a thirty million year gap between *Archaeopteryx* and the next oldest known bird. From the Lower Cretaceous period of France has come the thigh bone of a goose. Hind limb bones from Roumania have been called *Elopteryx*, and are believed to be from an ancestral cormorant. From Cambridge in England have come to light the bones of a pigeon-sized sea-bird named *Enaliornis*. Also from the Cretaceous period of Sweden have come a pair of primitive flamingos named *Scaniornis* and *Parascaniornis*. To date Cretaceous deposits in Europe and the Americas have yielded up twenty-four species of fossil birds including the well-known *Hesperornis* (western bird) of which there are at least seven specimens representing two or more species – one of which was more than six feet long.

9 FLIGHTLESS FISH-EATERS

Hesperornids were flightless fish-eating birds somewhat on the general pattern of a loon. *Ichthyornis* ('fish bird') was another of this period, eight inches in height and looking in size and shape something like a modern gull or tern. There is still learned argument as to whether or not these latter two

The yellow-crowned night heron is an infrequent visitor to Canada though it has been reported as breeding on Lake Erie.

had lost or still retained the reptilian teeth which would have greatly aided them in fish catching. One specimen of *Hesperornis* appears to have had some teeth. Certainly *Hargeria*, somewhat similarly formed and also found in the Cretaceous shales of Kansas, had no teeth. Both of these birds lived on or beside the huge inland sea which occupied much of North America one hundred million years ago. This sea, the last great sea of the North American continent, extended from the Gulf of Mexico to the Arctic Ocean through the present-day Prairie provinces, the Yukon and Northwest Territories. It survived for millions of years with a warm tropical climate.

In June 1965 bones of *Hesperornis* were excavated from the banks of the Anderson River in the Northwest Territories by Dr Dale Russell of the National Museum of Canada. Preserved in a Cretaceous deposit, seventy to 120 million years old, these ten fragmentary bones are the earliest known evidence of 'true birds' (*Neornithes*) in Canada. Only a month later Dr David Bardack of the University of Illinois also found the bones of *Hesperornis* in the Vermilion River formation in Manitoba. By the end of the Cretaceous period then, birds had differentiated at least to the extent shown by *Elopteryx*, *Scaniornis*, *Hesperornis*, and the twenty-one others – all aquatic birds. Here at least, at the water's edge, speciation amongst the birds was well under way. Speciation is the process of fine adaptation to a particular environment and specific way of life which is the secret of each creature's success and which renders it unique. It is extremely likely that this same process was also evolving and adapting new species for life on land during the same period, but we have little positive knowledge of them, nor as yet, any clear fossil evidence such as we have for the aquatic forms so nicely preserved by their ancient watery habitats.

With the advent of the Tertiary period the stage was set for great geographical and evolutionary expansion of the avian line. North America during the Eocene became covered by wide-spread tropical, subtropical and warm-temperate forests. Subtropical forests found along the Pacific coast

The white pelican is an early bird, little changed in millions of years. The bird breeds in BC, *Alberta and western Ontario.*

extended as far northwest as British Columbia and eastward to Wyoming. With the coming of the Oligocene the warm, moist climates of the Eocene became cooler and drier. Grasslands replaced forests. In Europe a similar situation existed. Birds of the wet Upper Cretaceous and the drying Eocene would now have to adjust to still drier conditions.

The origin of new species, that subject upon which Charles Darwin enlightened us in 1859, involves the development of new adaptations by a creature in order to exploit or survive changes in its environment. The species must change or adapt in order to survive. Darwin pointed out that the price paid by any animal which becomes so specialized as to be no longer able to cope with changes in its environment, is extinction. Thus, from such avian ancestors as we have seen in the Jurassic and the Cretaceous periods, came about in the Tertiary period the wealth of variety in form, colour, shape, size and habits of our modern birds. Formed by the catalyst of ever changing climatic events, they moved outwards from their simple origins in time and geography, expanding to fill every niche and cranny wherein today's birds are found.

Darwin's evolutionary theory recognized the significance of certain commonly observed phenomena and for the first time related them to explain 'that wonder of wonders, the origin of new species upon this earth,' as he wrote in *The Origin of Species*. Basically he saw that variation exists amongst the individuals of any species; that animals tend to overproduce, leading to intra-specific competition for territories, mates, and food. This competition creates a struggle for existence. Because of the observed variation in form or behaviour, some are better adapted to survive this competition than others. The survival of the best fitted is a natural process of selection in which the less fit tend to die off early leaving few or no descendants. Those fortuitously fitted for whatever changes and pressures are at work in their environment survive to reproduce their kind, and pass on their favourable adaptations. Darwin assumed that evolutionary change was necessarily a slow process. However, new light has since been shed on the subject.

Ancient anhinga from the tropics often visits West Coast sites.

43

10 REVEALING DIVERSITY

Hugo DeVries, a Dutch botanist, coined the term *mutant* for what had previously been called a 'sport' or 'freak.' Working on plant breeding experiments with two colleagues in 1900 he rediscovered the 1865 work of the Austrian, Gregor Mendel, who has been called the father of the modern science of genetics. Genetics is that branch of science which studies the mechanism by which characteristics are passed on from generation to generation. Mutations, as DeVries defined them, are abrupt genetic changes, usually minor but almost always harmful, which appear in newborn young. Occasionally however, such a mutation bestows some survival value on its possessor and allows some rapid evolutionary change. A recent example is the European house sparrow which was successfully introduced into North America at New York in 1852. From there it has spread over much of the continent to become a common and familiar bird to the farmer and city-dweller alike. Today, a short 121 years later, it shows distinct evidence of having *evolved* some climatic adaptations. House sparrows taken from wet Vancouver Island and placed beside those from New York are darker and larger. Those from dry Death Valley in California are lighter and smaller. In this regard the transplanted house sparrows have come to resemble some other native birds which show similar adaptations in size and colouration to extremes of wetness and dryness in their ranges. There are many contributing factors to the evolutionary process but Darwin's theorem aided by the discoveries of the geneticists appear to reveal the basic mechanism.

In the larger view the phenomenon of adaptive radiation can be taken to explain the evolution of all the world's birds from the single ancestral species to which *Archaeopteryx* must have been close. We speak of adaptive radiation when a number of animals, each being a separate species, reveals similarities in anatomy and behaviour traceable by scientists to a common ancestry. More usually the term is used to recognize the flowering from some single ancestor of a whole group of present-day species and subspecies such as are found within a taxonomic family or genus. By this process, although the originator is usually lost to extinction, its basic body plan and mode of life are retained by its descendants in a variety of modified forms.

This principle of adaptive radiation is nicely demonstrated by the waterfowl of the family *Anatidae* – ducks, geese and swans. Although worldwide in their distribution they owe much of their success story to the march of evolutionary events in North America. The continent now plays regular host to forty six of the world's 224 species. Around the basic and familiar anatid pattern of flattened bill, long neck, heavy body, short leg and web foot can be seen a considerable amount of specific variation which allows each species to fill its particular ecological role without undue competition and without having departed too far from the basic shape and form which renders them all easily identifiable to us as ducks, geese or swans.

No family of birds has been more successful and opportunistic in historic times than the *Anatidae* and it is therefore not surprising that it should have evolved in the past such a variety of species and subspecies around the basic water-living pattern of its ancestor. Nor is it surprising that it has been able to withstand the tremendous human pressure exerted upon it in the form of habitat destruction – mainly wet land drainage – and, of course, hunting. In the Americas the birds have adapted to differing climatic conditions from the Arctic tundra to the tropics, from the ocean swells of the Atlantic and Pacific to the fresh-water sloughs of the Prairies and the beaver ponds of our boreal forests. Their food preferences now run the gamut from the purely vegetable through every shade of variation to the fishy protein diet of the mergansers. Nesting varies between the shallow scrape (really no nest at all) of some high Arctic geese to the re-use of old woodpecker holes high in trees favoured by the wood duck, hooded merganser, bufflehead and goldeneye. By no means are our waterfowl restricted to the cattail marshes of popular belief.

Double-crested cormorant, spreading its wings to dry, probably achieved its present appearance about fifty million years ago.

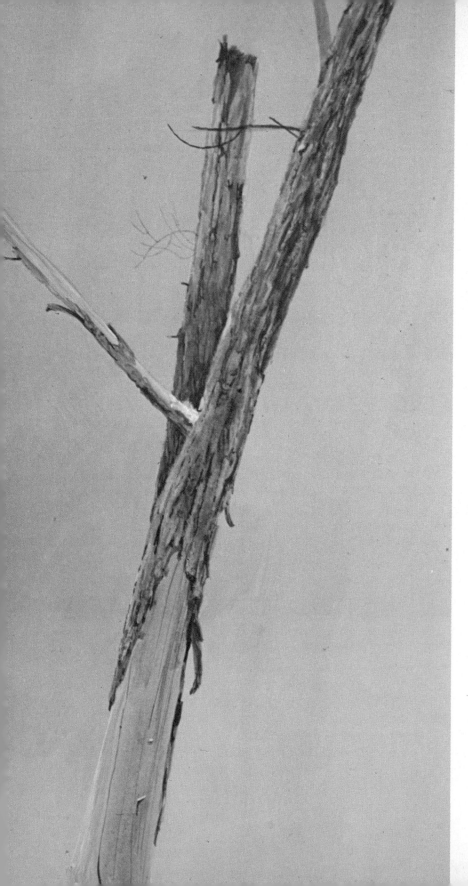

Taxonomists have arranged them into seven subfamilies which are divided into twenty-four genera and further divided into the forty-six species. Seven of these are further divided into more than one subspecies or race. This arrangement is intended to recognize the unique adaptations each has made to its specific or subspecific way of life. (It is worth remembering that only at the species level are the taxonomic differences recognized by the birds themselves. Subspecies can readily interbreed and do so when individuals are brought together artificially in collections. In the wild, being geographically separated, they rarely do so.)

11 A VARIETY OF FORMS

A quick look at the main features of this family will reveal its diversity. The swans are the giants of the waterfowl world and are distinctively long-necked and white plumaged. The mute swan has been added to the North American avifauna by introduction from Europe and has since gone wild of its own accord. They are almost entirely vegetarian. The geese include the widespread Canada goose, a creature so variable in size that the largest and smallest geographical races are in fact the largest and smallest geese in the world. *Branta canadensis maxima* was thought to have become extinct about 1920 until rediscovered by Dr Harold Hanson of the Illinois Natural History Survey in 1960 amongst wintering flocks near Rochester, Minnesota. Individuals of this race are reputed to weigh as much as eighteen pounds. Descendants of the original wild population had also survived in captive and semi-captive flocks in sanctuaries, parks and zoos – their large size having been wrongly attributed to their semi-domesticated state. Today their offspring are being used to restock suitable areas in their former range. *Branta canadensis minima*, the smallest subspecies, is a mallard-sized Canada which nests on the snow- and ice-bound shores of the Arctic's Bering Sea.

The turkey vulture is an ancient bird with some characteristics that link it to storks and cormorants.

47

The tree ducks are a long-legged tropical genus adapted to perching in trees on the shores of ponds and lagoons around the Gulf of Mexico and throughout the middle-American tropics. No one has satisfactorily explained why, on at least two occasions in recent years, flocks of the fulvous tree duck, a normally non-migratory species, have left their normal range to undertake suicidal northward flights. They have come up the Atlantic seaboard in the fall to arrive off New Brunswick (Grand Manan) and then swing inland up the St Lawrence River. In 1962 one surprised Ontario duck hunter shot one just east of Toronto.

The surface-feeding ducks are a large group which includes the mallard, undoubtedly the world's best known duck. The striking green head of the male and the familiar up-ending manner of feeding – orange legs wiggling – are familiar to us all. Less well known is the fact that most domesticated ducks are descended from this bird. The diving ducks on the other hand do not up-end. Their legs are placed so far back on the body that they walk on land only with difficulty. Theirs is the ability to dive deeply and gracefully to feed using their large webbed feet and half opened wings to 'fly' underwater. Invertebrate aquatic animals play a much more important role in the diet of the divers. The bluebills or greater and lesser scaup are the best known of this group. The cocky little ruddy duck is Canada's only representative of its subfamily and known as a breeding bird mainly to Western Canadians. It represents the 'stiff-tails' so named for the male's courtship habit of steaming around slough or farm pond like a diminutive tugboat with the tail held vertically.

The mergansers – usually called fish-ducks by the hunters – are the main protein eaters of the waterfowl world and for that reason are not highly prized by the gourmet. Their bills are thin and laterally compressed with tooth-like serrations to enable them to hold their slippery prey. There is something prehistoric about the appearance of the mergansers, perhaps their snake-like necks and serrated bills evoke in us images of the long gone hesperornids.

One species we have lost to extinction and the slim evidence we have of its passing for once suggests that man played little role in its demise. The Labrador duck (*Camptor*

hynchus labradorium) was the sole representative of its genus. Its breeding range is thought to have been in Labrador. It wintered on the Atlantic coast from Nova Scotia south to New Jersey and perhaps Chesapeake Bay. The last record of a living bird was on 12 December 1878. The Royal Ontario Museum and the National Museum of Canada each have a single preserved specimen.

12 THE ICE AGE COMETH

Such is the diverse character of this family. Because of their high adaptability, they have, through the process of adaptive radiation, evolved from an unknown progenitor the wide variety of forms, exploiting the wide variety of habitats in which we find them today.

The earliest known evidence of the family *Anatidae* in North America is a left humerus, excavated by Dr Loris Russell, chief biologist of the Royal Ontario Museum, in 1955 in the Wood Mountain formation in southern Saskatchewan, and believed to be from the Miocene epoch – ten to thirty million years ago. It resembles that of a modern goose. Dr Russell's goose establishes the true geese (*Anser*) in Canada, to which by this time they had spread from Europe.

Flightless birds are all believed to have had flying ancestors. In the case of the penguins they share affinities with the petrels of the order *Procellariiformes* whose fossil record also goes back to the Eocene. The common ancestor of modern penguins and petrels must have been some yet undiscovered dweller of southern shores and oceans back in Cretaceous times. Adaptations amongst flightless birds are all for swimming, running or hiding and examples can be found in a variety of different orders, ancient and modern. Some birds have in fact abandoned flight whenever and wherever they could adequately maintain themselves upon land or water. The largest of all living birds, the ostrich of Africa, is one such. Weighing more than 300 pounds with a height of eight feet he is but a pale shadow of the prehistoric moas (*Dinornithidae*), twenty-two species of which have walked the landscape of New Zealand as recently as 500 years ago.

The majority of avian fossils belong to the last ten million years of evolution during the Pliocene and Pleistocene epochs. From the period starting with the Lower Jurassic to the end of the Pleistocene, paleontologists have now described more than 800 species from their fragmentary fossil evidence. However, Pierce Brodkorb of the University of Florida, who has made a lifelong study of avian evolution, has estimated that 1,634,000 species, including those still extant, have been involved in the evolutionary process of genesis and extinction. Thus our whole knowledge of avian evolution depends upon a very small portion of one percent of the process. These fossil fragments, however, provide little windows opening upon the avian past, through which the paleontologist can glimpse strange and often bizarre species long gone from the earth together with some which appear somewhat familiar. What they have seen must illuminate the whole process.

Evolutionary expansion, both of numbers and kind, reached its high-water mark in the Pliocene. This epoch saw the emergence of many species which still fly today. Brodkorb estimates that 11,600 species were living at the end of the period. The Pleistocene which followed was to prove rigourous and destructive both to birds and the benign habitats which supported them. Four great glaciers were to advance and retreat across much of Europe and North America. Landscapes and their plant cover would be vastly changed. Migrations would save many species but climatic extremes would change with greater speed than many slow-to-adapt birds could keep pace with. This was to be a period of retrenchment, rapid evolution and extinction. The great age of expansion for birds was past; they would now become a dwindling class. Mammals and man were on the ascent and would begin to replace them.

Modern Canadian birds re-occupied a bulldozed postglacial landscape following a pattern which continues to this day. If one looks at the flora and fauna of, say, today's Arctic islands he will find species of plants and animals which are adapted to survive the long winters, cold temperatures, sparse food resources and generally rigorous conditions of Arctic living. Many birds occupy their Arctic territories only during the short summers when they can conduct their breeding activities. They must migrate to the south ahead of each returning winter in order to survive. Thus it was with the same plants and animals in southern Canada as the last glacier retreated. Within 7,000 years habitats suitable for the support of most of today's species had developed. They moved in from south, east and west. But 10,000 to 15,000 years would pass before southern Ontario would support the climate and attendant plant cover that now attracts such southern species as the great egret, prothonotary warbler and cardinal. The northward re-invasion takes the form of a linear progression of species each anxious to colonize new territory as it becomes available. Yet each species is obliged to await the development of habitat suitable to support it.

The spread into Ontario as recently as 1901 of a southern bird like the cardinal is taken by some scientists as plausible evidence of continuing climatic amelioration.

The paleontological story properly ends with the beginning of the written historical record. On the Canadian east coast, the arrival of Jacques Cartier and his ships in 1534 brought the curtain down on prehistory. Two hundred and forty years later the landfall on the coast of British Columbia of the Spanish explorer Juan Perez in 1774, likewise ushered in the start of the historical period in the west. Others were to follow and in their journals and letters appear mention of the birds and other wildlife they encountered. In many cases the species recorded, often with names transmuted and incorrect, were being seen by Europeans for the first time. The wealth of bird life offered a ready food source to the Europeans as it had already done for the indigenous natives for tens of thousands of years. The newcomers, however, had guns and a monumental disregard for the long-term wellbeing of the resources they exploited. Their eyes were upon more immediate and tangible goals. From this point in time onwards, the future of birds would depend, not on natural forces alone, but upon the actions of men.

D. H. BALDWIN

PART THREE
UNCERTAINTIES OF A LIFE ON THE WING

The male bluebird swept down from his perch atop the old apple tree to attack the newcomer – a stuffed bluebird. The live bird repeatedly flew at the intruder, uttering a harsh chattering note and making a 'clopping' noise with its bill. Finally it landed on the stuffed 'rival' and pecked at it again and again until some of the cotton stuffing fell out. After a few more passes it flew back to its tree-top perch and began to sing – at first softly; then the full, rich warble.

What had come over this famed symbol of peace and happiness? The answer is simple – yet complicated. It is spring and all birds are driven by a combination of chemistry and tradition to ensure the survival of the species. The male bluebird had established a territory, his place in the sun, which he would, for a few weeks, defend almost to the death, against all other male bluebirds. In that area, if things went

A male Canada goose upends himself as part of the courtship ritual performed in front of the females. The geese nest on land – usually near water – in a depression in the ground. It is lined with sticks and usually given an inner lining of down.

according to plan, the male and female would court, mate, build a nest and raise a brood of four or five young bluebirds.

After the winter hiatus, when most Canadian birds are in the southern United States and the Americas, the rush of migration begins. As the first migrants arrive, often in flocks, they soon seek their own territory. Old males sometimes return to the same place year after year, a fact proved by bird banding. If another male has claimed the territory there will be fights and squabbles until one male drives the other out. Large numbers of males fail to return each year, and their places are taken by young males.

The size of the territory that the male stakes out varies with the species. In her classic studies in the *Life History of the Song Sparrow*, Mrs M. M. Nice found that the sparrow's territory varied from one-half to one and one-half acres. The snow bunting, an Arctic nester, varied from one-half to seven acres. With larger birds like hawks and owls, the territory may be much larger – from several acres to many square miles, in the case of the golden eagle. Birds that nest in colonies often settle for a square yard or so. Leslie M. Tuck in *The Murres* describes how murres stake out a territory: 'There is a great deal of jostling for position on the ledges when the birds first settle in. . . . The birds parry each other's bills, slash at each other . . . after the birds have been on the cliffs for some time, fighting seems to be restricted to cases where there is interference with an occupied nest site.'

Territory may be defined as any defended area; however, this is, for practical purposes, a limited area defended by a bird (usually a male) against other males of its species for a part of the breeding season. The functions of territory are thought to be to assist in pair formation, to furnish food during the nesting period and to spread the species over a broad area thereby increasing the chance of survival.

The question – why do birds sing? – has intrigued man for centuries. Many ornithologists are of the opinion that the chief function of song is to advertise the location of the singer – to warn off rivals and to attract potential mates. Bird song is defined by Margaret Nice as 'a sustained, more or less uninterrupted repetition of one or more notes conforming recognizably to a constant specific type.' Most Canadians have listened to the *cheerily, cheery* song of the familiar robin. But few think of the caw of a crow or the honking of a goose as singing, yet these are the functional songs of those species.

Most birds sing for a short period only in the spring, and then most actively in the early morning and evening. There are exceptions, such as the red-eyed vireo, which seems to sing from dawn to dusk. One song sparrow sang 2,305 songs during a fifteen-hour day.

One of the most spectacular modes of singing is the 'flight song' uttered usually by the male during flight. These songs are given by meadowlarks, ovenbirds, and other species.

Besides songs most species have one or more calls, which may be given by both sexes. The calls have a number of functions – warning, attracting the attention of the young, announcing the position of one mate to the other and others not understood by man.

If birds are going to pair and reproduce they must be able to recognize their own species and their own and opposite sexes. Nobel laureate Konrad Lorenz showed that young birds normally learn to recognize their parents at an early age by a process the behaviourist calls imprinting. In one famous experiment Lorenz substituted himself in place of the

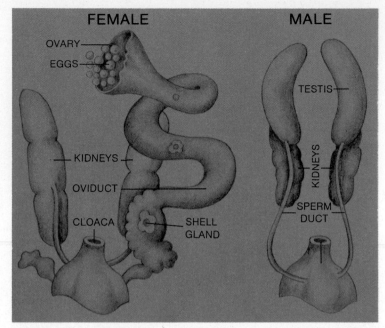

A male blue grouse displays the yellow eye wattles and the red air sacs of its courting plumage. The air sacs are bare spots on the neck that the bird can inflate; at the same time it puffs out an ornamental ruff of white feathers. Most kinds of grouse also perform an elaborate courtship dance with tail and wings spread. Another species, the ruffed grouse, produces a booming sound called 'drumming' during its courtship. For many years the manner in which the bird produced the sound was in doubt; some thought the bird beat against a hollow log with its wings. Slow-motion film has shown, however, that the bird cups its wing, draws them sharply down and swiftly up again; the drumming sound results from the rapid change in direction of the cupped wing. The reproductive systems of a typical male and female bird are shown in the diagrams (above). Both sexes have but one external orifice, the cloaca. Sperm manufactured in the testes travels down the sperm duct and through the cloaca of the male into the female's cloaca. Within the female, eggs which have started to form in the ovary are fertilized in the oviduct. At the shell gland in the oviduct the egg picks up yolk, egg white and the rigid shell of calcium. Birds lay varying numbers of eggs according to the species; many kinds of birds lay only a single egg, others as many as twenty.

The little gull, smallest gull in Canada, builds its nest near water and usually lays one to three eggs. This gull was considered a visitor; a 1962 report confirmed it breeds in Canada.

The bald eagle constructs its nest on a rocky ledge or in the highest branches of a tree near water. As the nest is used and added to year after year, it grows to immense proportions.

The red-eyed vireo builds its neatly styled nest in trees – usually deciduous, at times in conifers. The nest is made from strips of bark, paper from a wasp's nest. Three to four eggs are laid.

The pine grosbeak's nest is a flimsy affair of twigs, rootlets and grass. Four or five eggs, turquoise in color, are laid each season. The nest is usually built in a coniferous tree.

The blue-grey gnatcatcher builds its nest in tall trees, sometimes choosing a branch sixty feet above ground. It is a compact nest made of vegetal matter tied together with spider webbing.

Cliff swallows plaster their nests to the sides of cliffs and, in cities, frequently on buildings and bridges. The nest is made of mud gathered by the birds and is often roofed over.

54

Canada goose builds its nest in a depression in the ground. The nest is lined with sticks and reeds. The female lays four to six eggs which both sexes incubate for about four weeks.

Osprey's nest is often built in dead trees or occasionally atop a telephone pole. The nest is used and added to every year. The eggs, white and mottled with color, number two to four.

The yellow warbler's nest is built in a tree or bush, some three to ten feet above ground. Looking large and bulky from the outside, the cup is neatly constructed of plant fibres.

The pintail builds its nest on the ground, usually in a concealed place but often on open land on the Prairies. The eggs, pastel green or buff in colour, number seven to ten a clutch.

The northern oriole builds a pouch-like nest, looking very like a woman's handbag. It is skilfully woven of plant fibres and twine. Four to six eggs are laid, chicks hatch in two weeks.

Wood duck usually nests in a hollow tree trunk but will adapt to local conditions, even to building a nest in the chimney of a house. The female incubates the eight to fifteen eggs she lays.

Defining
a niche for every species
of land and sea birds

mother bird and the sight of young ducks paddling after their swimming 'mother' has been seen widely on TV. The matter of sex recognition seems to be through visible differences in appearance and through behaviour and voice when the sexes are similar. Most small birds mate for the first time the year following their birth; herring gulls take three years to mature.

Various kinds of behaviour help in bringing together males and females of a species. The male may sing, display plumage (the tail of the peacock is one of the most garish displays) or other structures, chase the female and sometimes fly against her. The female may answer the male with calls, approach the male in a 'coaxing' manner with body flattened and wings fluttering or communicate her interest by simply entering the male's territory.

When the female has wandered into the male's territory – attracted by his singing – she will be challenged. Her response of passive submission reduces the male's aggressiveness. There may be sexual pursuits and various displays. In some species, such as the bluebird and the cardinal, the male may feed the female in a ritual called courtship feeding much like the candy and sweets exchanged by humans.

Each species of bird occupies its own 'niche,' a pattern of behaviour that is uniquely its own. Part of a bird's niche is a location – a place in which the bird is likely to find conditions and food most to its liking. Warblers forage for insects atop the tallest trees of the woodlands. Pigeons often perch on high branches but nest lower down, chickadees hunt for food on low bushes and various kinds of woodpeckers frequent the mid-levels of trees and bushes. Thrushes, including the familiar robin, are ground feeders in the main, hopping about gathering worms and insects. On a rocky coastline, the highest levels will be occupied by petrels – when the birds are not at sea. On the next level down perch the cormorants and murres, both large birds which display their awkwardness on land. One level down reside the puffins, comical looking birds with their giant bills of brilliant colour. Just above the high tide mark live the guillemots, oystercatchers and related species of shore birds. The lordly eagle nests in trees atop the cliffs or rocky pinnacles. The number of eggs a bird lays (opposite) *is partially a function of the species' vulnerability – those birds most preyed upon lay more eggs so that their numbers may be replenished. Birds which can adequately protect themselves lay the fewest eggs.*

56

ABOVE: *PUFFIN* BELOW: *BLUEBIRD*

ABOVE: *MURRE* BELOW: *TERN*

ABOVE: *DOVE* BELOW: *PLOVER*

ABOVE: *GULL* BELOW: *PHALAROPE*

BELOW: *CEDAR WAXWING*

BELOW: *AMERICAN BITTERN*

BELOW: *CANVASBACK*

BELOW: *LOGGERHEAD SHRIKE*

BELOW: *CANADA GOOSE*

BELOW: *HOUSE WREN*

BELOW: *AMERICAN COOT*

BELOW: *COMMON FLICKER*

Twenty-one days in the life…

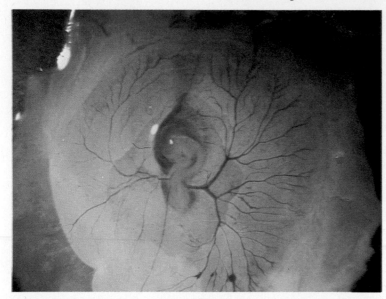

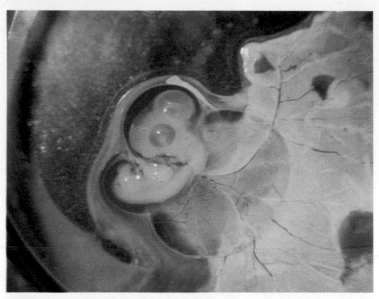

A chicken embryo in the fourth day after fertilization shows the major brain divisions already forming, the leg buds which will develop into legs and wings, and blood vessels leading to yolk.

The fifth-day embryo displays a rudimentary beak, a prominent, pigmented eye, a prominent bulge of the midbrain. Wings and legs have developed into recognizable forms by this fifth day.

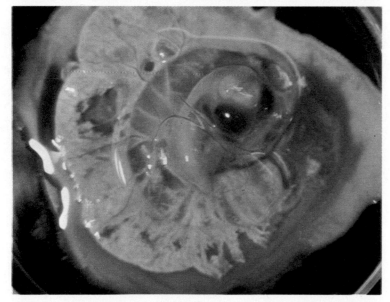

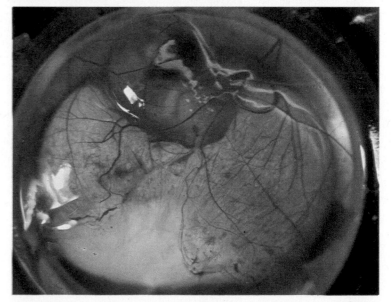

Nine days after fertilization the chick embryo is still enclosed in the amnion and displays most prominently its large, pigmented eye. The chicks hatch after about twenty-one days of incubation.

The embryo on the twelfth day is still enclosed in the fluid-filled amnion and rests upon the yolk sac. By this stage in the embryonic development the bird's eyes and wings are clearly defined.

58

...of an unhatched chicken egg

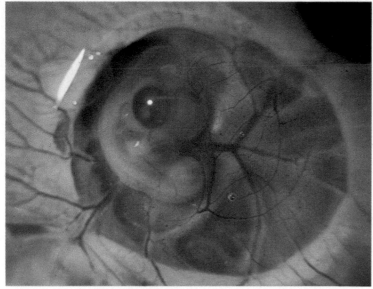

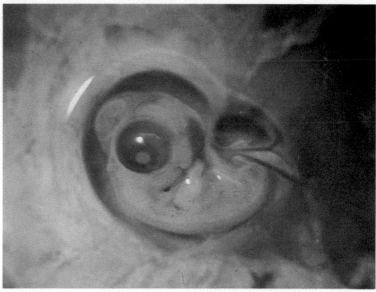

Still enclosed in the fluid-filled membrane (called the amnion) the sixth-day embryo shows little change from the fifth day. The embryo has grown somewhat and features are more easily seen.

The seventh-day embryo, still enclosed in the amnion, shows a smoother contour of the head. The chick's wings and legs show prominently. Note pronounced development of the bird's beak.

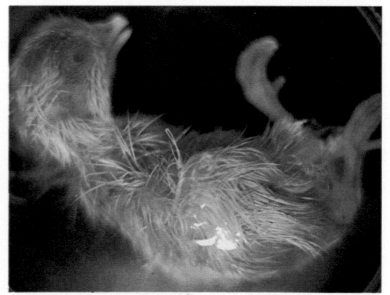

The embryo in the twelfth day has been removed from the protective amnion to show the beak, eyes, wings and legs. Feathers are mere buds; the white spot at the end of the beak is the egg tooth.

A fifteenth-day embryo has been removed from the amnion and covered with water to show the size and extent of its feathers. The bird also has been uncurled from its position in the shell.

13 COURSING OVER THE MARSH

Some of the most spectacular courtship activities are the 'nuptial flights' of waterfowl. In his classic *The Canvasback on a Prairie Marsh*, Albert Hochbaum, former director of the Delta Waterfowl Research Station in Manitoba, writes: 'Now in swift, straight flight, now twisting, diving, turning, towering, the two birds course over the marsh, the hen always leading, the drake shadowing her every move. Many times during the flight the hen may rise sharply out of a steep dive or break abruptly to one side, the male speeding on for many yards before checking to follow again.'

Whooping and sandhill cranes do a remarkable 'dance' which is regarded as part of their courtship behaviour. While dancing the cranes 'use their legs as springs, their wings as a balance, usually springing upward and slightly backward.' A spectacular performance when performed by two whooping cranes, which stand almost five feet tall and have a wingspread of about seven feet.

Most small birds have a relatively simple courtship behaviour. For example, the snow bunting male at first threatens every snow bunting that invades what he regards as his territory. However, if a female snow bunting refuses to retreat, the male changes his approach, spreading his wings and tail to show their conspicuous colours and then runs away from the female. The female's reaction is usually passive and over a period of a few days a bond forms.

After birds are mated they usually remain together during the nesting season. However, in species raising more than one brood per year, a change of mates may take place. Careful banding studies of common terns show that they retain their mates during the following season in about ninety percent of possible cases. There is a 'surplus' of both males and females available to replace an individual if for any reason it leaves its mate after mating. An experiment in New Jersey

A new-born white pelican breaks free of its egg.

followed a pair of indigo buntings. After mating the male was removed. By the next morning the female had found a new mate. The male was removed nine times and nine times the female procured a replacement in a short time.

The selection of a nest site is poorly understood by students of birds. A few species, notably the larger birds of prey such as eagles or peregrine falcons, may use the same nest for many years, adding more nesting material each new season. Some species, like the bluebird and chickadee, may use the same nest for successive broods during the course of a single breeding season. In some species (grouse, pheasants, shorebirds) the female selects the nest site; in other species (starling and house sparrow) the male appears to select the site; or it may be both sexes (doves, chickadees, jays and crows).

The selection of a site may take several days or even longer. The bluebird has an involved ritual, initiated by the male. He flies to a possible nest site – a nesting box, an old woodpecker hole, or a natural cavity in a tree – and flutters near the entrance hole, warbling a low, soft song. The male may perch at the hole, fly off, then perch again. The female may inspect the site, looking in and perhaps entering for a few seconds. Then they may fly off to check another site. The visits soon become more frequent and one or both may carry nesting material and drop it in the entrance hole. Finally one morning the female will begin carrying material to the site in earnest. In a few days, usually three to seven, the nest will be completed. As the season progresses less time is spent in nest building and a nest may be completed in one or two days.

Nests of different species vary from merely a scrape on the ground to the carefully woven nests of the orioles. The function of a nest is to protect the eggs and the subsequent young birds. There is great variation amongst species as to whether the female, the male or both sexes build the nest. The male house wren may build 'dummy' or 'cock' nests, often filling all available nesting holes in his territory. The male mourning dove brings materials, but the female alone builds the nest. In species such as kingfishers, swallows and most woodpeckers, both sexes share equally in excavating for the nest. The male frigatebird builds the nest, while the female supplies the material.

Birds nest in a great variety of locations. Some build no nest, and lay eggs on the ground or rocks – nighthawk, auks, guillemots; some nest on or near the ground – horned lark, song sparrow, marsh hawk; some dig shallow holes – most shorebirds and gulls; others dig burrows – kingfisher, bank and rough-winged swallow; some nest in bushes – catbird, brown thrasher; others nest in natural cavities – wood duck, screech owl, starling; others create their own cavities – woodpeckers and nuthatches; some build nests in trees – warblers, crows, vireos; still others build nests in or about buildings – phoebes, barn swallows, house sparrows.

The actual shaping and nest building by a robin has been detailed by F. H. Herrick in *Wild Birds at Home:* 'The female brings her load of dead grass or stubble to the nest, then settles on it and goes through a moulding movement, in which she vibrates her wings and stamps her feet. After moulding for five or ten seconds, she turns in the nest through six or seven degrees and repeats the process, continuing until she has turned completely around from two to four times. As building proceeds mud is added . . . the hole is moulded as if by a potter's wheel. An additional arrangement of material is effected by the bill . . . The lining is made of grass . . . which is moulded by the turning process.'

Nests vary in size from the tiny cup of the hummingbird to the large, bulky nest of the eagle which may be twelve feet across. The brown-headed cowbird avoids the chore of nest building by laying its eggs in others' nests.

The laying of eggs is synchronized with the building of the nest. Some species begin laying the day after the nest is completed; others may wait a few days. In birds that nest early in the spring, cold weather may inhibit egg-laying. Most small perching birds lay at the rate of one egg per day, usually laid in the early morning. Not all species operate on a twenty-four hour laying schedule. A number of owls, gulls and hawks lay eggs on alternate days; eagles may space their eggs as much as five days apart.

Goggle-eyed pair of green herons gawk at the stranger approaching their nest. The chicks are altricial – they require close parental supervision in almost all their activities for about one month before they leave the nest.

14 EGGS VARY IN NUMBER

The number of eggs laid by different species varies from one to about twenty. A single egg is laid by most penguins, petrels, shearwaters and by some auks and sunbirds. Hummingbirds lay two eggs. Most small birds in Canada lay from four to six eggs, although chickadees, wrens and nuthatches lay from six to thirteen. Most ducks and gallinaceous birds (grouse, pheasants) lay from six to fifteen eggs. Sometimes more than one female duck or pheasant may lay in the same nest and twenty to thirty eggs will result, but these so-called 'dump nests' usually are not attended and the eggs do not hatch.

Bird's eggs vary in length from about one-quarter inch in some hummingbirds to about thirteen inches in the now extinct *Aepyornis*. The majority of bird's eggs are oval-shaped, but there is considerable variation. Many birds lay white or near-white eggs, however the majority of birds have coloured eggs, either a solid colour or with various, often elaborate patterns. Those species that lay their eggs in a scrape on the ground usually have blotched, patterned eggs which blend in with the surrounding habitat. Everyone knows the robin's egg is blue, as are the eggs of most other thrushes.

When the clutch is completed the eggs are incubated. Incubating is simply applying heat to the eggs. Incubation may be by either female or male or both. Most birds develop incubation patches in the skin of the ventral abdominal wall a short time before incubation begins. The major change is the loss of feathers in the area, allowing the bird to apply the warm skin directly to the eggs. Usually only the sex that incubates develops an incubation patch.

Then follows a period of time from about eleven days to almost twelve weeks referred to as the incubation period.

Common murre nestling huddles for protection in its nest.

65

Ornithologists determine the incubation period from the time of the laying of the last egg in the clutch to the hatching of that egg.

In most species the eggs are only incubated part of each day and throughout the night. However in those species in which both sexes incubate, the eggs may be covered all the time. Most of the small songbirds in Canada have an incubation period of about thirteen to eighteen days. During the incubation period some males may feed the female while she is sitting on the eggs, thus extending the time she may sit without seeking food. Bluebirds, cedar waxwings and cardinals regularly engage in this behaviour. Some species, such as grouse and grebes and loons cover the eggs when the female leaves the nest. This serves to keep the eggs warm and also to hide them from the sight of predators.

For years it was thought that the incubation period of the brown-headed cowbird was only ten days. Recent investigations have proven the cowbird young hatch in eleven or twelve days. This shorter-than-normal period is thought to give the parasitic cowbird a headstart over the young of its host, usually a warbler or sparrow. Young cowbirds may throw the young of its host out of the nest.

Sometimes eggs do not hatch for a variety of reasons. One bobwhite male was reported sitting on a nest of thirteen eggs from 18 July to 7 October without apparent discouragement.

Birds are said to be either precocial or altricial, depending on the relative development at the time of hatching. The young of precocial species are covered with down at hatching and a short time after hatching they are able to run about. Young birds of some species may be heard peeping in their shell before hatching, for example curlews, plovers and some species of waterfowl. Birds with precocial young include the geese, ducks, cranes, rails, gallinaceous birds, shorebirds and the ostriches.

The young of altricial birds are wholly dependent on their parents' care for several weeks after hatching.

Tousel-headed kingfishers scold with a raucous rattle.
Overleaf: *Quizzical long-eared owls view the scene.*

66

The stage of development of precocial birds just after hatching may be compared to that of young altricial birds when they are ready to leave the nest, however their plumage is less well developed. Quails may fly within a week or ten days and grouse within two or three weeks; ducks and geese do not usually fly until they are about ten weeks old.

Growth of precocial young is slow at first when they are not able to easily find food, but it accelerates as they become more adept.

Young precocial birds respond quickly to the parents' calls as soon as they are hatched – a vital response if they are to survive and escape from predators. A. C. Bent described newly-hatched Prairie chickens as struggling over one another to get to the mother when she gave her *brirrrb brirrrb* call, but freezing to a motionless pose when she gave a sharp, shrill call of alarm. Young piping plovers will remain motionless for many minutes on hearing the alarm note of the parent. They blend in so well with the sand and pebbles of their beach habitat that you could be standing a few feet away and not see them.

Ornithologists in Alaska have put forward the theory that adult shorebirds may leave the nesting area and start their southward migration only weeks after arriving on the tundra to avoid competing with their precocial young for the limited food supply.

Young of species which nest over or by water, such as rails, black terns and gallinules, may tumble into the water soon after they are born. Ducks and geese, which often nest back a distance from the water, lead the young to the water as soon as they are able to walk and spend most of their time on the water from then on. Some hole-nesting ducks, such as the wood ducks, hooded mergansers and common golden-eyes, must entice their young to jump from the nest into the water or land below. Once one has jumped the others in the brood usually follow quickly, sometimes knocking one another off their precarious perch at the entrance to the nesting cavity.

An immature common tern stands shakily on its bright pink webbed feet. It breeds in every province except BC.

70

Gulls and terns are somewhat between the precocial and altricial types. Parent gulls feed their young for several weeks until they are able to fly, but the young may have left the nest a few days after hatching.

Precocial birds pick up their own food, but at least initially the parent aids in finding it. The young bird may pick up a pebble, a stick or some other object at first, but soon learns to discriminate between edible and non-edible items.

15 MASTER ACTORS AT WORK

When an enemy (including man) approaches the nest or young, some birds attempt to distract it by simulating an injured bird. The killdeer is a master of this – spreading and dragging its wings and tail, calling and moving slowly away from the intruder. If followed it gradually increases the distance between it and the pursuer until finally it suddenly flies up and off to circle the area until danger has passed.

In contrast to the young precocial birds, the young altricial birds are hatched in a very immature or helpless condition and require a prolonged period of care and feeding in the nest until their feathers develop, their temperature is regulated and they are able to fly. Newly-hatched they are blind, nearly or entirely naked and almost cold-blooded. They squat on their bellies in the nest, their wings offering some support. Their legs are able to pull away vigorously, thus ensuring that the young do not get entangled in the nest material. The eyes are merely slits. Some peep when they are hatched, others when they are a day or two old. Altricial birds have an egg tooth or egg breaker located on the upper bill with which they cut the eggshell, in a process called

Gaping mouths of three young robins almost obscure their bodies. The robin, a kind of thrush, is probably the best known bird in Canada. Stories about robins getting slightly drunk from overindulging in too-ripe berries are not folklore but true.

Coping with the bald eagle

Two young ospreys (left) wait patiently for a parent to return with dinner. The osprey is a kind of hawk and excels at taking fish alive. It soars in great circles above the water some fifty to 200 feet up until it sights its prey. It hovers momentarily and plunges down, feet first and wings half folded. Often the bird disappears beneath the surface with a mighty splash only to reappear in a few seconds with the fish irrevocably pinioned in the sharp talons (above). Like the owls, the osprey's outer toe is reversible so that the bird can grasp its catch with the head pointing forward. The bald eagle is the osprey's most persistent tormentor, frequently harassing the smaller bird until it drops its catch. Though never found very far from water, the osprey is one of the most widely distributed birds in the world. So successful has the bird been that it has established colonies on remote volcanic islands where no other species of hawk has managed a foothold. Apart from the two polar regions and other locales that are constantly frozen, the only places the bird is not found are New Zealand and Hawaii. The bird migrates from Canada to winter in South America. Ornithologists disagree on whether the osprey is endangered; some believe the bird is losing in numbers, others assert the species is in no immediate danger.

75

The problems—and solutions—of fishing on the wing

The skimmers are the only birds with the lower mandible longer than the upper and the black skimmer (opposite) is the only species of the family found in Canada. The bird flies close to the water ploughing the surface with the long, lower mandible. When the bill strikes a fish or crustacean, the upper mandible closes and the bird has snared its meal. As it must skim the surface to get its food, the black skimmer has a distinctive flight pattern in which the wings never flap below the horizontal. On close examination, it may be seen that the upper mandible has one sharp cutting edge, the lower two. When the skimmer closes its mandibles, the cutting edges fit neatly together creating a tight fit to hold the squirming fish. Skimmers nest in colonies on sandy beaches, creating a shallow depression by rotating their breasts in the sand. Here they lay from two to five eggs. The young are precocial – ready to move about the nest as soon as they have dried off after hatching. At hatching, both mandibles are of the same length and the lower does not start to grow until the birds are full grown. The black skimmer is the largest species of its family and is an occasional visitor to the Atlantic provinces. The skimmer fishes mainly in the early evening and night when fish and shrimps come to the surface. To protect their sensitive eyes, absolute essentials for nocturnal fishing, the bird has vertical pupils which can be narrowed to slits to prevent damage by the sun during the day.

Bonaparte's gull (below) is, like most gulls, an excellent flier and can pluck a fish from the water with great dexterity. Cruising along above the water, the bird looks for prey. When sighted, the bird dips down, occasionally almost jolting to a stop from the impact, and then lifts off with its victim firmly clasped in its bill. Most species of gull are disconcertingly alike in appearance but the Bonaparte's may be distinguished from other black-headed gulls by the white leading edges of its wings which flash out in contrast to the darker trailing edges with every wingbeat. Though often referred to as 'sea gulls,' gulls are seldom found far away from land. The petite little kittiwake of northern Newfoundland is the only species regularly found out of sight of land. Gulls are primarily coastal birds and are such adaptable creatures that any sizeable body of water offers them sufficient reason to populate its shores. Though they prefer animal food and fish, gulls will eat almost anything. Inland, they will follow the plough for the worms and grubs it turns up. When large insects swarm, as locusts do, gulls congregate from miles around to feed. In the nineteenth century, a horde of 'crickets' – grasshoppers, really – descended on the Mormon settlers' grain crops in Utah. Gulls swarmed to the area and destroyed the insects in sufficient quantities that a harvest was possible. The Mormons commemorated the birds' help in saving the crops and gulls are almost revered in Utah.

'pipping.' The time required for the young to break its way out of the shell varies from fifteen hours to several days in larger birds.

The first response of the newly-hatched young bird is its feeding reaction. Any sound or jarring of the nest causes the young to raise its head and open its mouth. The lining of its mouth is generally red, with a border of white or yellow, providing a distinctive target for the parent bringing food. Both parents usually share the task of feeding the young. The parent usually shares the food between two or more young. The young that call the loudest and can reach the highest are fed first, which should ensure that the hungriest are fed first. However, all the young are not uniformly strong or of equal size and often the runt of the brood dies before the rest leave the nest.

The food of young birds is almost entirely animal matter, regardless of the fact that the adults may be mainly seed-eaters. Caterpillars, earthworms, grasshoppers, moths and other adult insects are staple food for young songbirds. Hawks and owls bring mice, rabbits and other prey to the nest, sometimes ripping it up for distribution to the young. Some species, such as the cormorants and waxwings, feed by regurgitation – that is, partially digesting the food before bringing it up in a soupy mixture to feed the young.

The rate of feeding varies considerably with the species and of course intensifies as the young (especially of song-birds) grow larger. The warbling vireo has been observed making forty-five trips to the nest to feed in one hour. Bluebirds have made more than 400 trips in a fourteen-hour day to feed a brood of four young. The bald eagle may make an average of four trips per day in a period of four days to bring fresh food to its nestlings.

Young birds in the nest may gain fifty to seventy percent of their hatching weight in twenty-four hours, and continue to grow at an even greater rate until they leave the nest. It is

Gaping wide, three young barn swallows wait to be fed. The bird breeds in every province and winters in South America. It is a particular favourite of Canadians since its return in April is a harbinger of spring.

reported that the young gain ten to twelve times their own weight in the first ten days and hence gain sixty to eighty percent of their adult weight by that time. Weight gains are retarded when feather growth accelerates.

Young songbirds begin to open their eyes when they are from one to four days old and apparently soon distinguish their parents by sight.

Near the end of the period in the nest the nestlings become increasingly active. They move about, stretch their wings and legs, preen their feathers, climb up on the edge of the nest and in the case of the hole-nesters (bluebirds and woodpeckers) look out the hole and greet their food-bearing parents. They also become increasingly vocal in their calls for food. The young of small songbirds may stay in the nest for from ten days to three weeks, the young of large raptors for several weeks. Just prior to leaving the nest the young seem to develop a sense of fear and an ability to escape danger – so essential to survival.

The young of birds that nest in holes or cavities usually remain in the nest until they are able to fly, while those of birds in open nests may leave (sometimes they are frightened and flutter out) before flight capability is fully developed. As a rule the young do not return to the nest once they have left. Some swallows are exceptions, and may return to roost for a few nights.

Nest leaving is a period of considerable disturbance on the part of both the parents and young. For some time the parents will continue to feed the young. If a second brood is undertaken the task of feeding the young falls to the male.

Like all perching birds this pine grosbeak can gobble berries as easily hanging upside down from a tree branch as it can right side up. It prefers to nest in coniferous trees but in winter and during migration it is more often found in and around shady deciduous trees, orchards and shrubbery.
Overleaf: *Digging in its heels, a young robin drags an unwilling earthworm from the ground. This bird is not yet fully mature and wears juvenal plumage. The spotted breast will become solid red when the bird reaches adulthood. The bird is typically found today in close association with man.*

while the female builds a new nest or rehabilitates the old one.

The young of most small songbirds are fed for a period of from four to six weeks. Some larger species (crows and ravens) may continue feeding for a much longer time.

The young undergo considerable development and maturing after they have left the nest. They follow one or both parents constantly and gradually learn to procure their own food. Ground-feeding species seem to become self-sufficient at an earlier age than such species as kingbirds which are flycatchers and take most of their food on the wing.

16 DO BIRDS 'LEARN'?

The question of how much teaching of the young takes place is contentious. But it seems that many young birds do learn by example. Anyone watching a family of kingfishers trying to cope with the problems of fish-catching must realize that there is some teaching involved. (Text continues on page 91.)

84

Another adaptation for defence is colour – in most species the male is more brilliantly coloured than the female and, thus, more likely to distract a potential enemy than is the inconspicuous female. The pair of painted buntings illustrate the differences between the male (above, left) *and female. In spite of its almost garish garb the male usually stays fairly well concealed within the foliage of its woodland habitat. In breeding season, the male displays himself on an open perch and sings a melodic song, half in encouragement to its incubating mate, half to frighten off intruders. In addition most males are larger than females; in most hawks and related species the female is considerably larger. Opposite: 'There's strength in numbers' seems to be the watchword of the Funk Island colony of common murres. This colony off the northeast coast of Newfoundland is estimated at one and one-half million birds. By massing together in formations like this the murres cut down on the chances of eggs or young being taken by maurauding gulls. The Canadian Wildlife Service now restricts visitors to the island (in fact, a group of three islands) so the murres are unlikely to fall victim to man's despoilation as did the great auk, a previous resident of the island which was eradicated in 1802.*

Camouflage for survival

The willow ptarmigan of Canada's Arctic adopt a camouflage pattern to make themselves inconspicuous in the tundra vegetation. Even with patches of snow on the ground the bird is hard to distinguish. In winter the mottled feathering is replaced with solid white so the bird tends to be invisible in all weather. The ptarmigans are almost unique among birds in having the entire foot – toes included – covered in feathers. Presumably this gives their feet a greater carrying power, a kind of snowshoe for getting around in snow. Ptarmigan mate for life and while the female incubates the eggs the male stands by and helps raise the chicks when they hatch. The chicks are precocial – they can move about on their own within an hour of hatching.

Overleaf: Three horned larks, almost perfectly concealed in the sere, dead grass at the base of the fencepost, are another example of nature's camouflage at work. So well do these small birds melt into their background that they feel safe in allowing a close approach before they flush. The larks spend most of their time on the ground, walking or running rather than hopping. They feed on animal and vegetable matter, insects, seeds and berries. This species is the only lark native to Canada and is found in the forested parts of all provinces.

During the first few weeks following nest leaving the young bird undertakes activities such as drinking, singing, 'playing,' bathing, fighting and sunning. Also they undergo their first real molt and assume their first-year plumage. Non-songbirds may retain their juvenal plumage for a longer period.

The number of broods or nesting attempts per season which a species raises or initiates varies with the species and with the geographical location. Most large birds make just one nesting attempt, although they may make a second one if disturbed early in the cycle. But small songbirds, like the bluebird may make as many as three attempts in the southern part of their range, while just one at the extreme northern periphery in Canada. In some of the more remote parts of Canada, especially the Arctic, weather conditions may be such that it is impossible for the birds to make even one attempt to nest. This happened recently when late melting of ice and snow wiped out attempts by many geese to nest. Sometimes a sudden and violent storm will destroy nests and eggs too late in the short season to allow another nesting attempt.

Relations between parent and young is best described as a reciprocal social relationship. The young bird gives distress calls when separated from the parents or the rest of the brood or when cold, hungry or restrained. Pleasure notes may be given in response to contact with its fellow nestlings.

There is considerable evidence to suggest that the adults of many species, for example most songbirds, doves, hawks and herons, do not recognize their own young. This has been demonstrated by a number of ornithologists who have transferred young birds from one nest to another. The transferees, either of the same species or a different one, are usually fed and accepted. An interesting reaction sometimes takes place when young birds are banded while still in the nest. The adult may see the band, 'consider' it as not essential to the nest and try to remove it. There are documented cases of adult birds carrying the intruding young out of the nest.

A woodcock in its 'autumn leaf' plumage huddles almost invisible on the woodland floor. The woodcock is one of the first birds to arrive back in Canada after its winter migration.

Nobel laureate Niko Tinbergen, of Oxford University, undertook a classic series of experiments to determine what triggers the feeding response in young herring gulls. He found that a significant factor was the red spot on the mandible of the adult. Using a series of cardboard models Tinbergen's researchers found that responses were reduced as much as seventy-five percent when the red spot was absent or moved from the bill to the forehead.

One of the most striking social activities of birds is the gathering together of numbers into flocks. Many species gather together in summer prior to the fall migration. The flying of Canada geese is a familiar sight as are the swarms of robins and blackbirds in September and October. Some species, such as chimney swifts, crows and starlings, gather at common sleeping areas; others, such as gulls, feed together. Black-capped chickadees form flocks in fall and remain together during the winter. A study showed the chickadees had at least sixteen different calls and songs which were used by individuals to communicate with other members of the flock.

In the definitive *The Birds of Canada* by W. Earl Godfrey, a total of 518 species are listed as occurring or having occurred in Canada. Of this number only a little more than ten percent occur right across the country from sea to sea to sea.

Some species which have been found nesting in all provinces and the territories are robin, hermit thrush, Tennessee and magnolia warblers, ovenbird, redwing, brown-headed cowbird, pine grosbeak, savannah, chipping and white-throated sparrows, common loon, bittern, common goldeneye, bald eagle, osprey, common snipe, herring gull, Arctic tern, great horned owl, short-eared owl, hairy and downy woodpecker, horned lark, raven, crow, bank swallow and boreal chickadees.

Still other species have an extremely restricted range in Canada: the blue-gray gnatcatcher is found in Ontario only; Ross's goose in the Northwest Territories; the cardinal in Ontario and Manitoba; the spotted owl in British Columbia; the prothonotary, blue-winged and Prairie warbler in Ontario; whooping crane in the Northwest Territories; the pygmy nuthatch in British Columbia; and the Carolina wren in Ontario.

JAMES WOODFORD

The terrible ire
of a threatened female

Honking a challenge, a female Canada goose inspires caution in a potential enemy coming near her nest. Usually the male stands guard while the female incubates the eggs; in this case the male was absent foraging for food. Canada geese nest near fresh water; this one was found beside a heavily used runway of an Ontario airport located on a lake. This is the best known and most widespread goose in Canada; it is wary and sagacious but easily tamed. Small domesticated flocks of the geese have been maintained at various places in the country. The birds stand about twenty-five to forty inches in height and range to about fifteen pounds in weight. The white cheek marks and long, black neck are a reliable guide to identification of this species. As with all waterfowl, the Canada goose is of ancient lineage and fossil bones of the bird have been dated to eighty million years ago in the Mesozoic era. Waterfowl were probably the first birds domesticated by early man and they have fascinated mankind ever since. They have been bred, harvested, eaten, painted and studied: the literature on waterfowl is more extensive than for any other kind of bird. All are swimming birds with comparatively short legs and webbed front toes. A few species are solitary but most waterfowl flock in migration, feeding and some even breed in colonies.

Sudden death

A wheelbarrowfull of common murres (left) represents one Newfoundland fisherman's daily catch of the birds. Diving for fish and displaying an underwater grace that makes their flight in air appear ungainly, the birds often pursue their prey to a depth of 280 feet; if they fish near nets they often become ensnared in the webbing of the nets and drown. "Turre pie," a common Newfoundland dish, is made from the bodies of drowned murres; turre, an approximation of the sound of the bird, is the Newfoundland name for the species. Though expert at 'flying' underwater the murre is an indifferent flier in air. It waddles along the ground to a high rock from which it launches itself into a glide and then flight. Flapping powerfully it stays aloft until it sights a school of capelin or herring for which it aims and dives. Underwater it 'flies' with ease.

A northern oriole (right), formerly known as Baltimore oriole, hangs dead in the crotch of a tree. Birds are often killed in this way: two branches of a tree get crossed and entangled in a wind. If a bird is perched on a branch when it snaps back to its proper place, the bird is crushed or strangled.

Hidden dangers

A common coot (left), *a marsh bird of all provinces except* NS, PEI *and Newfoundland, hangs impaled on a barbed wire fence. It was probably caught when it tried to fly between strands of the wire. Other birds are often caught in wire fences when two strands of wire, twisted by the wind, snap back into place snaring the bird by neck or feet. If the bird is lucky, death comes fast.*

Although man represents the single, most dangerous threat to the life of any bird, natural hazards must be met as well. This herring gull (right) *attempting to land in the tangled vegetation along a lakeshore, impaled itself on a stiff shaft of a dead bullrush. Totally unable to free itself, the bird would have died if the photographer had not broken the reed and released the bird. The bird shook its injured wing once or twice, then lifted off and flew away.*

PART FOUR
THE FACTS AND THEORIES OF MIGRATION

Ask any Canadian – even one with a jaded attitude toward nature study – how far birds migrate. 'A long way,' will likely be the answer. How long? 'Mexico, maybe South America. A long, *long* way.' The certainty is there, even if we are unimpressed with it.

Bird migration is an obvious phenomenon in Canada, especially in spring. From the arrival of the earliest waterfowl onwards, different species fairly explode, one after another, upon the scene. Arrivals are said to occur in waves. It is most impressive east of the Rockies, where the extreme one hundred-degree swing between summer and winter temperatures provokes an urgency not seen on the Pacific coast. The culmination is the high tide of warblers.

Actually, of the estimated 8,580 species of birds in the world, only little more than a third migrate at all. Furthermore, Roger Tory Peterson calculates that only about fifteen percent of the world's birds indulge in this dramatic north-and-south, long-distance movement we in Canada associate with migration.

Migration references therefore occur throughout Canadian literature as devices to measure passage of time or to create mood. Each spring the first robin's arrival is announced on the front page of newspapers. Usually a local naturalist is quoted on previous records, and when to expect other arrivals.

Native peoples of Canada were even more conscious of migration than we are. The Cree Indians call April *Niska peesim* – month of the goose; October is *Pi a oo moo peesim*, – month of the migration south. Even *Pinésiwak*, the Thunderbird spirit of the Saulteaux Indians, lived in the south during winter, and spent spring and summer in the north.

The term migration is derived from the Latin *migrare* – to go from one place to another. Generally it now describes a kind of round trip made by birds that breed in one area, and fly to another area during the post-breeding period.

Thus chickadees, juncos, pine grosbeaks and finches mi-

Flying high over Cap Tourmente, Quebec, a pair of snow geese head southwest from their Arctic breeding ground toward the southern US or Mexico where they will spend the winter. Thousands of snow geese stop off here regularly during migration.

grate in winter from the upper altitudes of the Rockies to the lower, from 9,000 feet to 4,000 feet. In one mile of flight they change habitat sufficiently to survive, while members of the same species in the more eastern part of their range may have to travel more than 1,000 miles south to effect the same change in environment.

On the other hand, Rocky Mountain blue grouse migrate *up* in winter. Their diet of fir buds and needles is assured even at higher altitudes, and by moving up they avoid predators which are forced to descend.

Heermann's gulls, which breed on islands off the coast of Mexico, migrate north as far as the lower BC mainland and southern Vancouver Island.

The snowy owl, one of the most magnificent and widespread Arctic birds, is periodically affected by drops in its staple diet of lemmings and mice. It moves south in what L. L. Snyder calls an attempt at migration, since few return in the spring to complete the migratory cycle.

The red-eyed vireo is a special case. Its range extends from Canada to Brazil and Argentina. Some remain year-round residents in the centre of this range. Some migrate south, while others come north to breed. After breeding, all return to winter with those that never left.

Most of what we know about migratory bird behaviour has been learned since the turn of the century, although the mystery of such goings and comings must have fascinated prehistoric people as well, for sketches of birds occur on the walls of caves inhabited by stone age man.

Homer made references to migration. So does the Old Testament; Job 39:25 reads: 'Doth not the hawk fly by thy wisdom and stretch her wings toward the south?' It is also mentioned in the Sanskrit *The Sacred Books of the East*.

Opposite: *A flock of swallows perching on a telephone line like so many clothespins assembles for its migratory flight to South America. Migratory birds of Canada and the northern United States tend to favour four principal routes which have become known as 'flyways' (two are shown* right), *mainly as an administrative aid for ornithologists. Actual migratory paths vary widely from species to species and in fact from individual to individual.*

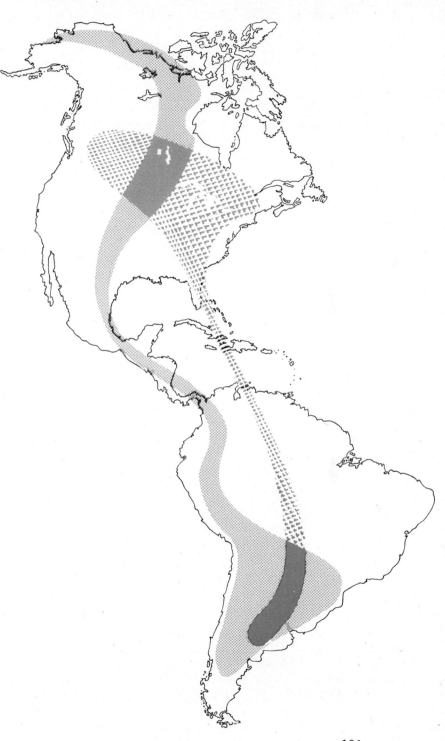

17 ARISTOTLE WAS WRONG

The notion that birds hibernated persisted for many centuries. Aristotle knew that many flew to warmer climates, but he also believed in transmutation, saying the summer robin changed into the winter redstart. Later, when trans-ocean migration was accepted as fact, it was thought that small birds hitched rides on the backs of bigger birds.

Early attempts at documenting migration included a famous experiment in eighteenth-century England to test the notion that swallows hibernated in mud at the bottom of ponds. Dyed threads were tied to swallows' legs to test the theory that immersion in water over a long period would wash out the dye.

Bird banding for eventual recovery in North America has become a highly cooperative venture between the bird banding office of the Department of the Environment in Ottawa and the United States Fish and Wildlife Service, and also between amateur and professional ornithologists.

Banders are licensed, and are supplied with serially numbered aluminum bands. As each individual bird is banded, the species, subspecies, date, weight, sex, and other pertinent data such as presence of parasites are recorded and turned over to the authorities.

Capture for banding must ensure the safety of the bird. Ground foraging birds like finches can be trapped with bait, and a cage with a trip or trick entrance. But more elaborate measures must be used to take other birds.

The Heligoland trap, once used to stock larders, is the oldest of these devices. It is simply a huge funnel of mesh enclosing several small trees or shrubs. Birds are chased into the trees and down the funnel until they are trapped in a box

A lucky birdwatcher might see the ultra-rare whooping crane stopping over in a Saskatchewan grainfield during migration. Overleaf: *The ring-necked pheasant, introduced from Asia, stays relatively close to home during the year.*

102

at the small, narrow end of the trap's funnel structure.

Boom nets carefully folded in front of small, mortar-like cannons, are attached to weights which are fired into the air. The weights arch over flocks of large birds like Canada geese which have been attracted with grain, and the net falls upon them.

Of all the latest capturing devices, banders are most enthusiastic about the Japanese mist net. Mist nets are made of fine black silk or nylon thread woven into a mesh measuring anywhere from thirty to thirty-eight feet in length, and from three to seven feet in height. The netting is hung loosely from horizontal lengths of twine. A bird flying into it stretches the mesh into a gentle trap, so that removal is easy and captives are seldom harmed.

Recovery, of course, is the aim of banding, and thousands of individuals must be banded in order to get one recovery. This is particularly true of smaller species. Ninety percent of recoveries are waterfowl and game birds reported by hunters.

Much knowledge of migration dynamics is gathered by naturalists in the field. Thousands of them throughout North America conduct counts of birds along migratory corridors and at known stopovers. There are so many expert field observers that estimates of numbers or unusual sightings are quickly supported or disputed.

Sometimes evidence turns up in unexpected ways. Trainmen in a shunting locomotive in Toronto found a snow bunting which had been banded in Greenland.

Small flashlights that eventually drop off have been attached to the legs of waterfowl in order to observe them during night migration. Birds are often dyed in vivid, unusual colours so field observers can quickly spot them. During the summer of 1973, a mating pair of snow geese were spotted near La Péruse Bay, near Churchill, Manitoba. They had been dyed brick orange by ornithologists studying the migration movement of this species at the Anahuac refuge in Texas.

Information concerning nocturnal migrants has been collected by studying the full moon through telescopes. Mathematical equations taking into account the relative position of the moon in its path, and the cone of observation which varies in size, are used to analyse counts of birds crossing the face of the moon.

18 TRACKING BY RADAR

Counts taken in this manner can be coordinated with counts taken elsewhere. During 1952, for instance, 265 observation stations in Canada and the US were manned by 1,391 observers from twilight, 1 October to dawn 5 October. Silhouettes of 35,407 birds were recorded, indicating the activity and direction of migration over the entire continent. No other systematic study aids so much in reducing all such observations to an equal comparative basis.

When it was discovered that blips or 'angels' appearing on radar screens were birds, another new device was quickly enlisted in the study. Little was known about the height of migratory flight, for example, until 1960-61 when I.C.T. Nisbet used radar to determine altitudes of migrants over Cape Cod.

Three or four hours after sunset, the radar showed most flights taking place between 1,500 feet and 2,500 feet above sea level. Later, in 1963, radar showed that many birds migrating at night flew at greater heights during a cloud overcast.

Single, twelve-second sweeps of radar beams are now recorded in slow motion on 35mm movie film. When the film is projected at a normal speed the viewer sees the pattern, direction, and spatial distribution of the flight.

Aural identification helps experts distinguish species in nocturnal migration – something radar cannot help determine. Nowadays parabolic reflectors with microphones at the center, tape recorders, and amplifiers raise the ceiling of reception to more than 10,000 feet.

Some of the most impressive facts about migration are those which document extraordinarily long journeys. The Arctic tern, a strikingly beautiful bird slightly smaller than

Snow geese are gregarious birds that migrate in vast flocks. Tens of thousands whiten the skies along their spring and fall route. Controlled hunting has rescued the species from near extinction.

a pigeon, with long wings and a deeply forked tail, travels the longest known distance in migration. Its breeding range is circumpolar, and its wintering areas comprise the south Atlantic, south Pacific, and Antarctic oceans.

In the west, the Arctic tern generally follows the coastline south, sometimes travelling inland in northern parts of the country. In the east it heads out across the Atlantic to the south coast of Europe, and then turns southward along the west coast of Africa. It continues southward along the coast. As the migrants approach the Cape of Good Hope, some birds round the cape and spread out over the sea as far as New Zealand. Others continue south to the edge of the Antarctic ice pack where they may encounter those terns that have migrated down the Pacific coast. Still others turn west from the cape and fly diagonally across the south Atlantic to the east coast of South America.

The Arctic tern's course is marathon in its dimensions. No other species breeds so abundantly in North America, and deliberately crosses to the old world. Some details of its route are still lacking. Its flyway south of California is still undetermined, yet it is accepted that it continues to the Antarctic.

One young Arctic tern banded 22 July 1927 at Turnevik Bay, Labrador, was recovered 1 October of the same year on the coast of France. Another, banded 23 July 1928 in New Brunswick, was recovered the following 14 November in South Africa.

The golden plover is another long-distance champion with an involved route. Its northern Canadian population migrates east to Nova Scotia and Newfoundland, then strikes south 2,000 miles across the Atlantic to South America. After wintering in Argentina, Uruguay, and southern Brazil, it flies northwest to Central America, up the Mississippi valley, over the Prairies, and up the Peace and Mackenzie river valleys where it finally disperses into its nesting grounds.

The western Alaskan population crosses instead to Hawaii, and then spreads out to various Pacific islands, some as far

Most sandhill cranes in the marshes and fields of the southern Prairies are passing through on their way to or from Mexico and Cuba.

south as New Zealand. They return in spring by the same route.

The bobolink, whose long, bubbling song is so closely associated with the meadows and fields throughout southern Canada east of the Rockies, migrates 6,000 miles between its northernmost breeding point and southernmost wintering ground in Argentina.

This trip is doubly impressive because it so closely follows the ancestral route between the north coast of South America and the US. The population that has spread into Western Canada could take a more direct trip through Mexico and Central America.

The rufous hummingbird nests in Canada from southwestern Alberta north to Alaska, and migrates about 2,000 miles to winter in Mexico. The rubythroat, which is the only hummingbird widespread in the east, regularly makes 500-mile trips across the open waters of the Gulf of Mexico when moving to and from its winter range in Mexico and Central America.

The blackpoll warbler – sometimes called the Arctic tern of the warblers – nests as far as the timberline in the district of Mackenzie. It migrates in a zigzag pattern, first southeast toward the Atlantic coastal plain, then southwest, then southeast again to island-hop across the Antilles to South America.

---

19 FAVOUR THE FLYWAYS

Migratory birds of Canada and the northern United States tend to favour four principal routes which have become known as flyways. These are the Atlantic, Mississippi, Central, and Pacific flyways. The flyway concept originated with early attempts to manage waterfowl. But birds do not read flyway maps; the continued use of the flyway concept is more to help ornithologists communicate – it is more an administrative device than a real map with pinpoint accuracy. It is now customary to speak of specific corridors which vary within these flyways according to species.

The song sparrow, which breeds throughout Canada, moves south all across the country. Harris's sparrow, on the other hand, migrates along a narrow route between the short grass Prairie and the eastern woodlands.

When the corridor followed by the whooping crane was finally found from the Wood Buffalo Park area of southern Mackenzie, through the Dakotas and Montana, Nebraska, and Oklahoma to the Aransas refuge in Texas, a major step was taken toward protecting the whooper, since residents and authorities along the way could be forewarned.

The looping shape of the Atlantic colony of the Arctic tern across the old world and then back up a direct north route is duplicated in many other species to lesser degree. Spring migration northward is always more rapid and straightforward. Connecticut warblers and the western palm warbler, for instance, swing across to New England in the fall, but fly north through the Mississippi flyway in spring. These loops may be an adaptation to prevailing winds.

Migrating birds are divided into nocturnal and diurnal groups. A few travel by day *and* night. Most of the smaller insectivorous species are nocturnal migrants, but swallows and swifts, which feed during flight, are diurnal travellers.

Hawks, eagles, and vultures also migrate by day, since they need to travel when thermals or updrafts occur. Thermals are bubbles of air which are heated by the earth. Dark, freshly worked fields are excellent generators of thermals. The thermals rise, and the birds ride the thermals, gliding from the top of one to another.

Updrafts are currents of air which are deflected by escarpments, ranges of mountains, or coastlines. Migrating hawks and eagles tend to follow updrafts. Thus definite migration routes have been established where unique landforms create the most favourable currents.

The most famous of these is Hawk Mountain, on the Kittatinny ridge in eastern Pennsylvania, which is within easy driving distance for southern Ontario bird watchers. Another less dependable observation spot is along the Niagara escarpment and near St Thomas, Ontario.

Some migrants flock and some do not. Even the manner of flocking varies. Loons often fly in lines, well apart. Waxwings and blackbirds form compact groups without formation.

The three-toed sanderling flies in close formation, without an apparent leader. Yet the entire flock can change direction instantaneously in some mysterious, beautiful way. Shrikes usually fly alone, and one ornithologist even feels that they defend aerial territory.

The most recognizable flocking pattern in Canada, of course, is the V-formation of our ducks and geese. Most people now understand enough about the principles of aerodynamics to conclude for themselves that birds in this flight formation are riding on the rising vortex of air created by the downstroking wings of the bird immediately ahead, which likely conserves energy. However . . .

The V-formation is often retained after landing on water. What use could it have here?

Vocal communication certainly may play a role in maintaining flock formation after dark, which may, in turn, facilitate orientation. Tape recordings of bobolinks, a nocturnal migrant, were played to captive bobolinks that were in a physiological migratory condition. The captives responded to the calls, often flying up and hitting the top of the enclosure.

Routes and destination may vary a great deal even within members of the same species. The red-eyed vireo has already been mentioned as dividing into three groups: those that stay put in the centre of its range, those that fly south to breed, and those that come north. The pintail duck may migrate from our potholes and Arctic marshes to the northern US, or as far as South America.

Departure times even vary according to age and sex. The youngest song sparrows and mockingbirds leave their nesting grounds first, then the females leave, and then the males depart. The young of many Arctic shorebirds go last instead of first. The male rubythroated hummingbird starts south in July, leaving the female to raise the brood.

Speed of migratory flight tends to be greater than ordinary cruising speed. Small nocturnal migrants – possibly helped by a brisk tail wind – have been clocked at an average of

All mourning doves move southward in winter, those breeding farthest north migrating farthest south.

110

Migrating north in the spring the golden plover generally flies up the Mississippi and across the Prairie provinces. Returning it takes a split route with many flying over the Atlantic.

Snow geese are one of the many bird species that do not follow a well-defined migratory 'highway.' In both spring and fall migration they appear in large numbers across Canada.

thirty-six knots by means of radar. One might guess that speed would increase in direct proportion to favourable winds, but not so. For a ten-knot increase in wind force, the ground speed of the bird increases only slightly more than three knots.

Most ducks and geese migrate at speeds between forty and fifty miles per hour. Bald eagles and golden eagles have been timed at about fifty miles per hour.

---

20 ALTITUDE VARIES

Flight altitudes vary according to species and weather conditions. Shearwaters, loons, grebes, and scoters fly within 200 feet of the water, and often just above the waves.

Radar checks over Cape Cod indicate that nocturnal migratory activity of smaller birds peaks at about three or four hours after sunset, and that altitudes vary between 1,500 and 2,500 feet. A few higher records were taken at 15,000 to 20,000 feet, and it was estimated that between ten and twenty percent of the migrants flew below the 600-foot level.

A migrating bird faces countless hazards, natural and man-made. The female in Fred Bodsworth's haunting little novel, *The Last of the Curlews*, is shot by a farmer while enroute with its mate to their Arctic breeding ground.

Skyscrapers, broadcasting towers, and airport ceilometers take substantial tolls. Lighted buildings tend to attract migrating birds, especially during rain, fog, or low overcasts. Ceilometers, which project a beam of light upward to the cloud level over a landing field, have been responsible for

The Arctic tern makes two spectacular journeys each year between the Arctic and the Antarctic. The northeastern populations in Canada begin by heading across the Atlantic.

major kills, but are now equipped with filters to produce blue or purple light which does not seem to attract birds so easily.

During one fall migration near Topeka, Kansas, a total of 1,090 dead birds were collected beneath a 950-foot television tower. Sixty-one species were identified.

In 1956 a whooping crane was killed when it flew into a high tension wire across its flight path.

One famous example of the effects of drastic weather occurred in 1907. Heavy snowfall and icing conditions forced Lapland longspurs down over an area of 1,500 square miles during their migratory flight to the Arctic. On two small lakes alone it was estimated that approximately 750,000 longspurs had landed.

Winds often force landbirds out to sea, and sea birds inland. Unusually heavy fogs cause some species to lose their bearings. Winds, perhaps even jet streams, are thought to be responsible for the large number of North American birds that end up in Europe each year, among them the pectoral sandpiper, buff-breasted sandpiper, black-billed cuckoo, robin, and Swainson's thrush. Few European species ever make it to this continent.

As yet, there is no generally accepted theory to explain why birds migrate.

The *northern ancestral home theory* suggests that all birds in the northern hemisphere were non-migratory in the days before the Pleistocene glaciers, when a mild climate prevailed. With a moderate winter, there was no need to migrate.

Then, with glaciation, northern hemisphere birds were forced south in order to survive. Later, as the ice cap receded, the original northern inhabitants returned. As the extremes between winter and summer developed, the rhythm of migration became hereditary. This concept, however, does not explain migration in parts of the world where glaciers could not have been the cause.

The *southern ancestral home theory* is the northern ancestral home theory stated the other way around, with one important variation. It drops glaciation as a root cause, and instead suggests that the ancestral home of all birds was in the tropics. As the seasons in the northern hemisphere developed into the nearly equal lengths we know today, pioneering individuals worked north in summer and back in winter, or were forced by population pressures to adopt such a pattern.

The *continental drift theory* is more recent. According to the notion of continental drift, southern and northern land masses split up into our present continents. Before this split, it is postulated, birds made short flights between breeding and feeding areas.

Continental drift gradually stretched these routes, and birds adapted to the ever-increasing distances. However, most geologists believe the continents separated long before birds began to migrate.

Nor are we much closer to knowing the external trigger for migration. One early theory suggested the signal was leaves turning yellow.

But it is not merely a seasonal change, or a depletion of food supply. Swallows, some flycatchers and warblers, and breed – is dependent upon enlargement of the gonads. One environmental factor proven to stimulate this recrudescence in many cases is the changing daily amount of light received by the bird, or the increase in the photoperiod.

The first significant proof of photoperiodism as a starter was provided by Professor W. Rowan in Alberta between 1925 and 1929. Working with captive slate-coloured juncos and crows, he gradually subjected them to increasing amounts of artificial light to simulate spring. Birds exposed to the longer day showed enlarged gonads; those experiencing the normal winter day did not. When released, those with enlarged gonads flew away to find a mate, and the others stayed.

21 FAT BUILDS UP

But increased light could not trigger the migratory mechanism in birds wintering south of the equator, as they must begin their journey in days of uniform, or even decreasing, daylight. A bobolink setting out from Argentina would have to be well into the southern US before a longer photoperiod could stimulate its gonads. One expert believes the effect of light is cumulative and not immediate. In addition, the breeding cycles of many birds – barn owls and sooty terns, for instance – do not conform to yearly light cycles.

A phenomenal build-up of fat reserves takes place in many species before migration. Fat takes up more than fifty percent of the weight of a hummingbird about to migrate, and between fifteen and forty percent of weight in larger species. On the other hand, tree sparrows do not build up such impressive fat deposits before migrating. Nor is fat necessarily burned during the great flight.

Temperature and humidity also influence the migratory impulse. The arrival of a cold front can stimulate movement southward in the fall, and ground northbound migrants in spring. As a consequence, many species have become known as weather migrants, and others as instinct migrants.

The greater yellowlegs is an instinct migrant. It travels

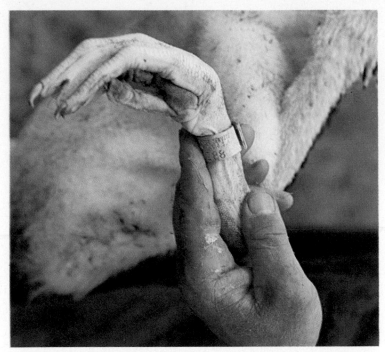

This white pelican (above) *will wear its aluminum anklet the rest of its life*. Opposite: *A seine net is being used to round up a flock of awkward young white pelicans for banding.*

bobolinks have been known to start south in July. Alternately, robins and bluebirds often press north into areas where food is scarce. Common loon yearlings migrate from the Arctic at the close of their first summer, but why do they remain in their wintering waters the first year, thus skipping the first migratory flight, only to join it the next year?

Changes in plumage, or molting, occur at definite times in relation to migration. Molting usually takes place before migration south, but in some longer-distance fliers, like the turtle dove and peregrine falcon, it begins in the breeding area, is postponed during migration, and resumed in the wintering grounds. Other species like the red-backed sandpiper (or dunlin) perform a pre-nuptial molt while working their way north, and a second molt in the wintering range.

Molting is brought about by a change in the endocrine balance, while the urge to breed – indeed, the ability to

between Patagonia and the Canadian Arctic, a total distance of as much as 20,000 miles, and hatches its eggs between 26 May and 29 May. The robin is a typical weather migrant whose arrival in a nesting area may vary by three weeks.

Many individual birds tend to return to the exact locality in which they were bred, and to the same wintering spot. Thus we come to the greatest puzzle of migration: how homing ability operates.

Homing ability has been documented time and time again in displacement experiments. For example, 220 Leach's petrels were once taken from their nesting burrows on Kent Island, off Nova Scotia, and were shipped away in various directions for release. The majority of them returned to their burrows. Some had travelled almost 500 miles, over half of them across open ocean. A Manx shearwater flown from Wales was released near Boston, and was found back in its nest twelve days later.

The remarkable nature of various attempts to thwart the homing instinct has been exceeded only by the results.

In Germany, two cages of starlings were shipped about one hundred miles by train. Someone had theorized that birds were able to home because they remembered twists and turns along their route. So one cage was placed on a phonograph turntable which was operated continually during the train ride. Therefore the starlings would have to recall all the revolutions of the turntable as well as the direction of the train. Most of the birds returned home.

A recurring theory suggests that homing ability has to do with a kind of built-in receptivity to the Coriolis force, which is produced by the rotation of the earth. Still another theory postulates a built-in compass that responds to the earth's magnetic fields.

The first experiments showing that birds are able to determine direction in relation to the sun's position were carried out in Germany by Gustave Kramer.

Kramer began studying a species of starling which is a diurnal migrant. He observed that during spring days, they oriented toward the northeast, and that during fall days they oriented toward the southwest. These were the directions in which they would normally migrate.

This gannet (above) *has been liberally splattered with red dye to make it readily identifiable even in the air.* Opposite: *Despite appearances the winking snowy owl is not being injured. This trap is one example of several used to catch birds for banding.*

Then Kramer built cages with six windows, each with a shutter. With most of the shutters closed he observed through a transparent plexiglass floor in the case that the birds were still able to orient themselves in the proper direction.

He began using mirrors to shift the angle of direct sunlight entering the cage. Each shift caused the starlings to shift their own orientation to an equal degree.

The sun, however, does not stay in the same place in the sky during the day, and each day its position in the sky changes. In six hours it changes its position by ninety degrees. Kramer theorized that a built-in time clock compensates for its changing position.

Another German, K. Schmidt-Koenig gathered supporting evidence for this concept by keeping homing pigeons in a series of rooms where a specified, artificial day-night cycle could be created. With one group of birds the light was switched on and off six hours before natural sunrise and sunset. With the second group the light was switched on and off six hours later than natural sunrise and sunset. With a third group, the light was switched on at sunset and off at sunrise, thus exactly reversing the normal light cycle. A fourth control group was exposed to the natural cycle.

Schmidt-Koenig theorized that if the pigeons had such an internal clock, it would be reset by the altered day-night sequences, and would therefore throw the orientation of the birds off to a predictable degree when they were released at random points.

He calculated that birds whose time clock had been advanced would deviate ninety degrees to the left of the control birds. They deviated seventy-two degrees. Birds whose time clock had been retarded, he figured, would deviate ninety degrees to the right, They deviated ninety-three degrees. Those whose time clock had been completely reversed would fly in the opposite direction, or 180 degrees away from control birds. They deviated 168 degrees.

This evidence was unassailable. However, it shed little light on how nocturnal migrants navigate. Two more Germans were to find the answer.

Franz and Eleanore Sauer began working with cages similar to those used by Kramer. They noted through the plexiglass bottom that warblers, who are strict night migrants, oriented toward their traditional direction of migration in spring and fall. On overcast nights, however, orientation became random.

The Sauers moved their birds to a modern planetarium where the appearance of the night heavens could be projected onto an overhead dome. When light was diffused across the dome, their nocturnal activity was random. But when an artificial spring night sky was projected on the dome in spring, they immediately oriented themselves toward their traditional northeast migratory direction.

S. T. Emlen, working with indigo buntings in another experiment in a planetarium, found that he could block out certain parts of the sky without confusing the birds. During the spring migration period, the northern sky alone was sufficient for the birds to find direction. They were even able to orient themselves correctly when the big dipper and north star were blocked out.

Celestial navigation, however, only shows how birds may generally find their migratory direction. Nobody knows how they are able to pinpoint goals.

Some diurnal migrants follow landmarks, of course. They may even deviate ninety degrees from their flight line in order to follow a coastline. Dr Albert Hochbaum, retired director of the Delta Waterfowl Research Station in Manitoba, suggests that such orientation is not explained by the notion of blind instinct, but that traditions of travel relating to patterns of landscape evolve and are transmitted.

So the phenomenon of bird migration still remains, essentially, a mystery. Whenever scientists get together and one presents a paper on the topic, it is always certain to generate great interest.

As recently as late 1973, Dr C. Romero-Sierra, of Queen's University, Kingston, Ontario, was presenting yet another theory at an international symposium in Poland on the biological effects of microwaves.

The theory as reported suggests that birds use their feathers to detect minute changes in temperature, humidity, and the earth's magnetic system. As temperatures drop in the fall, the bird's feathers tune into the local magnetic field in such a way as to create discomfort for the bird. As this discomfort worsens, the bird attempts to find a direction of escape that lowers and eventually eliminates the discomfort.

Studies at Queen's and at the National Research Council in Ottawa show that the properties of bird feathers change with temperature and humidity. Research has been done using microwaves to scare birds away from airports, and accounts for the portion of the theory which suggests that feathers act as sensitive receiving antennas in electomagnetic fields. Time may eventually tell.

WAYNE MCLAREN

This metal decoy is used by hunters to attract the birds. Before restrictions were placed on hunting, the snow goose was in danger of serious depopulation.

PART FIVE
ENDANGERED BIRDS AND NEW ARRIVALS

The Ipswich sparrow will never inspire a best-seller, rate a moment on television news, or stir a public outcry on its behalf. It is the ultimate in avian simplicity. Six inches long with dun-coloured plumage that blends into its sand-dunes habitat, and an undistinguished song, the Ipswich begs anonymity. It has none of the regal bearing of the whooping crane, which enjoys such an excellent press; none of the slender grace of the Eskimo curlew, so eloquently chronicled in Fred Bodsworth's novel, *The Last of the Curlews*. Who has even *heard* of the Ipswich?

Yet it deserves our concern for one compelling reason. Like the crane, the curlew and hundreds of other birds, this small sparrow is in danger of vanishing from the earth.

It breeds in one place only: tiny Sable Island, ninety miles off the Nova Scotia coast. There, the bird scrapes a shallow

The great auk (left) once flourished along the north Atlantic but was totally destroyed by unrestrained hunting. The passenger pigeon (right) darkened North American skies with its vast numbers but was gunned and trapped to extinction by 1914.

depression in the ground, lines it with grass and lays four or five blue-white eggs speckled with reddish-brown. For centuries the sparrow has followed this pattern, surviving many threats to its existence. Its annual flight against powerful winds to this solitary nesting place requires strength, persistence and pin-point navigation. Over the years, as well, man has introduced in turn: rabbits which stripped Sable's vegetation, rats which came off ships and killed the rabbits, cats imported to kill the rats, then dogs and guns brought in to quell the cats.

Throughout all this the Ipswich sparrow has prevailed. Estimates of its numbers in the last decade have ranged from 4,000 to a mere fifty-eight (bird counting is not yet an exact science). But naturalists agree on one point: the Ipswich is now an endangered race, for man and nature are threatening it in new ways.

Sable Island is low and sandy. Almost imperceptibly, the sea is rising, as well as eroding the sand. Some day, many decades hence, the sparrow's only nesting ground may be submerged.

Its winter home is in more immediate danger. The sparrow

winters along the Atlantic coast from southern Georgia to Massachusetts (it was found and named at Ipswich, Massachusetts, in 1872). New holiday resorts are relentlessly eating up land and driving wildlife off the seaboard. The US Fish and Wildlife Service has urged private owners of coastal land to leave their sand dunes in a natural state – an essential condition for the sparrow – and perhaps some owners will. Perhaps, too, Canada will take steps to protect Sable Island and its inhabitants. With the Ipswich sparrow, as with approximately 300 other birds today, survival depends mainly on the whim of the world's leading predator: man.

(The disappearance of the Ipswich sparrow is now considered to be less imminent than was thought. Most ornithologists now believe the Ipswich is merely a subspecies of the savannah sparrow, a race in no danger of extinction.)

Directly or indirectly, carelessly or deliberately, we are methodically killing off the other creatures of this earth. Since 1600, when records became reasonably reliable, some 150 forms of birds have ceased to exist. What is most alarming about these statistics is the increasing rate of extinction. About ten species or subspecies (called 'races' in ornithology) died out during the 1600s; about twenty in the following century; another twenty between 1800 and 1850; about fifty from 1851 to 1900, and another fifty since then. In the last century, therefore, we have lost an average of one form of bird nearly every year.

---

22 NUMBERS OBSOLETE

'Approximately' 300 is the most accurate available count of those presently in peril, partly because numbers become obsolete almost before they are published, partly because there is no standard measure of endangerment. When *is* a

A long-time favourite of falconers, the noble peregrine falcon is one of the world's swiftest birds, capable of killing airborne prey with a single blow of its taloned feet.

species endangered? In their book *Last Survivors*, naturalists Noel M. Simpson and Paul Geroudet, offer a theoretical rule-of-thumb: the point 'when losses [from whatever cause] so exceed recruitment that the total population begins to approach the minimum number necessary to sustain a viable population.' This threshold number varies enormously from one species to another, the authors point out. Locale is a critical factor too. A small but stable population on an island is nevertheless vulnerable; a majority of extinct birds were island-dwellers.

Frank Walden, special advisor to the fish and wildlife branch of Ontario's Ministry of Natural Resources, rates a bird as endangered when 'there is scientific evidence that the population is declining, and an explanation of the reason.' In 1973, for example, Walden was not persuaded that the osprey was in trouble in Canada (there may be 8,000 to 9,000 of them across the country). But because pesticides are sharply restricting its rate of reproduction, the Canadian Wildlife Federation includes the osprey in its official list of eight endangered birds, along with the Ipswich sparrow, bald eagle, prairie falcon, peregrine falcon, Richardson's pigeon hawk, greater prairie chicken, whooping crane and Eskimo curlew.

The CWF list, however, makes no mention of Canada geese, but a distinguished writer-scientist team, Lorus and Margery Milne, in their recent book, *North American Birds*, sound the warning for two races of Canada geese. Dr W. Earl Godfrey, curator of birds at Ottawa's National Museum of Natural Sciences, and author of the original endangered list for CWF, now believes the greater sandhill crane should be listed. This tall handsome bird once roamed freely across the Prairies. Guns and settlement drove it steadily into northern latitudes and now, so-called civilization is hemming it in.

In addition to the clearly endangered species, says Dr Godfrey, several others are in precarious straits in Canada, although less so elsewhere. They include the bobwhite, red-bellied woodpecker, Acadian flycatcher, prothonotary warbler, blue-winged warbler, and hooded warbler in Ontario; a dwindling population of great cormorants on the east coast; a tiny colony of canyon wrens in the southern Okanagan valley of BC.

Dr Godfrey is not the only scientist to say, in effect, 'Don't wait until a species is nearly gone before getting alarmed.' In 1971 Kees Vermeer, a biologist with the Canadian Wildlife Service, warned that at least ten nesting colonies of white pelicans have disappeared from Canada in the past twenty years, through direct interference from man. Although twenty-six remain, mostly in the Prairie provinces, they won't last long at this rate.

Other naturalists fear that *all* our hawks, owls and eagles are in danger, through pesticides which get into their food chain. And H. Albert Hochbaum, writer-in-residence and former director of Manitoba's famed Delta Waterfowl Research Station, is alarmed at the drop in North America's duck population, caused by hunting.

To the well-meaning authorities who tread cautiously in citing endangered species ('If we load the list, we'll cheapen it,' says Ontario's Frank Walden), concern for all hawks and ducks may seem ludicrous at this point. Sadly, though, mankind has shown a talent for wiping out species that lived by the millions, or even billions. Extinction can come with quick and awful finality.

Man is not *totally* responsible for the vanished or vanishing birds. Extinction is a natural part of evolution. Species live at the most only a few million years, before evolving into others or dying out entirely. Certain creatures are doomed through overspecialization, the inability to adapt to change, or through some natural catastrophe such as holocaust or ice age. Thus, just as the dinosaurs vanished from the earth, the teratorn – a gigantic bird of prey with a sixteen-foot wingspan – vanished from the skies about ten million years ago.

But of the 150 forms of birds lost since 1600, fully three-quarters have been wiped out by man. Part of it was through destruction of habitat: draining swamps, cutting down forests, ploughing up grassland, building dams, cities and resorts. Part of it was through hunting for food, feathers, sport or in so-called 'pest control.'

Until well into this century, hunting amounted to undisciplined slaughter. The dodo – so often joked about that many of us regard it as a myth – is a classic example. There once *was* a dodo: a fat harmless bird, waddling around the island of Mauritius in the Indian Ocean some 400 miles east

Above: *The regal and powerful golden eagle, once widely distributed in the mountainous regions of the world, has become increasingly rare due largely to over-vigorous hunting. 'Sportsmen' often considered the bird competition for small game such as squirrels and rabbits; in fact, where it is allowed to prosper, the bird is a ruthless controller of small rodent populations. In Asia the golden eagle was trained to hunt for game larger than that taken by hawks and falcons; it was once the symbol of Rome's power and the Latin name for the bird,* Aquila, *is the name of its genus even today. Golden eagles are long-lived birds and once having established a nesting site, return to it year after year.* Opposite: *The bald eagle, once a commonly sighted bird in all parts of Canada, is now seen seldom except in remote areas of the Yukon and* BC. *The bird's numbers have declined alarmingly in recent years. Part of its disappearance may be blamed on* DDT *ingested with the poisoned fish the bird eats. Another reason may be the destruction of tall trees in which the birds nest. As cities and towns encroach upon the surrounding countryside, most of the bald eagle's favourite nesting sites disappear. The bird can kill prey with its powerful talons but prefers to scavenge for fish along the beach.*

of Madagascar. It was about the size of a turkey, dark brown with tiny wings, uptilted white tail feathers and a big curving beak similar to a parrot's. Having nothing to fear until western man arrived in the sixteenth century, the dodo laid its single large egg upon the ground.

---

23 DODO EXTINGUISHED

Portuguese sailors (who called the bird *duodo*, or simpleton), Dutch sailors and British sailors came off their ships, ignorant, rapacious and hungry. They clubbed the naive slow-running birds by the hundreds, and ate them. Pigs and rats from the ships ate the eggs. Before the end of the seventeenth century, the dodo was gone.

It took only a little longer to wipe out the great auk. Once it abounded along the Atlantic coasts and islands, from Newfoundland and Iceland as far south as Florida. Some thirty inches long, black with a white underbody, the auk was a strong swimmer and diver – but flightless. Once on shore, where it nested, it was an easy catch. Jacques Cartier on his first voyage in 1534 salted down five or six barrels of the birds for each of his ships. By about 1830 only a few remained in Europe, where museums were now clamouring for them. And so one morning in June, 1844, driven by a museum reward of 100 kroners (about thirty dollars), two men went ashore on an island near Iceland and killed the last two auks on earth. They ran but uttered no cry and offered no fight, for they were gentle birds.

The black and white Labrador duck was next. It lived along the Labrador coast and the Gulf of St Lawrence, until the feather hunting, egg stealing and shooting of the eigh-

The pale piping plover almost disappears against the white sandy beach it inhabits. Her nest is an unlined depression in the sand. Although it still breeds in the southwestern lake regions and along the east coast it has become rare in the Great Lakes region where it was once common.

teenth and nineteenth centuries finished it off. The last known survivor was killed near Long Island, New York, in 1875.

In the long recital of man's inhumanity toward other creatures, no tale is more shocking than that of the passenger pigeon. It was a trim handsome bird about seventeen inches long, with slate-blue back and head, red breast, and shoulder feathers tinged with bronze, green or purple according to the changing light.

One autumn day in 1813 the artist-naturalist John James Audubon watched a seemingly endless flight of pigeons blackening the sky above him near Evansville, Indiana. As he followed the road all day, the pigeons flocked above him undiminished. Audubon put his scientific mind to work – two birds to the square yard, travelling at sixty miles per hour – and reckoned there were 1,115,136,000 birds in that flock. Around him on the river banks, men and boys shot down pigeons by the hundreds. Yet how could anyone seriously deplete such numbers?

It was easy, really. By 1855 New York City alone ate 300,000 pigeons a year. All over the United States and populated Canada, professional trappers, shooters and pickers flourished, speeding their catches to market aboard the new-fangled railway trains. Three nesting locations in Michigan alone were said to have yielded 2,400,000 adult birds and a thousand *tons* of squabs. This taking of the young hastened the birds' extinction. Also, between 1866 and 1876, twelve million brooding pigeons were slaughtered, which meant that their young ones died from abandonment if they too weren't taken for meat.

By the early 1900s only a few pathetic captives survived. The last passenger pigeon died in a Cincinnati zoo in 1914. The last Carolina paroquet – a lovely little green and gold parrot – died there too, four years later. Paroquets (also shotgun victims) had a fatal habit: when a flock was fired upon, the curious survivors wheeled back toward the guns to investigate the commotion.

By now, for the fathers of our country and the one next door, the pattern was clearly established: kill not just for food but for fun. After all, was not nature everlastingly bountiful? The *Red Data Book*, now the world's foremost document of endangered creatures, published by the International Union for Conservation of Nature and Natural Resources, sums it up: 'In our late historical times, such conservation forces as have been available have resembled a weak unarmed police force in a town where looting is going on.'

In 1833 on the eastern end of Labrador's St Lawrence shore, Audubon saw large flocks of a slender, dappled, long-billed shore bird, the Eskimo curlew. With other naturalists, he delineated its lifestyle: it nested in the Canadian north above the tree line and wintered as far south as Argentina and southern Chile. Twice a year the little curlew made this exhausting journey. By thousands, perhaps millions, the birds moved up and down the flyways, against all the hazards of nature. Then, enter a new one, named man.

'The slaughter was almost unbelievable,' wrote Fred Bodsworth, in *The Last of the Curlews*. 'Hunters would shoot the birds without mercy until they had literally slaughtered a wagonload of them, the wagons being actually filled, and often with the sideboards on at that. Sometimes when the flight was unusually heavy and the hunters were well supplied with ammunition their wagons were too quickly and easily filled, so whole loads of the birds would be dumped on the prairie, their bodies forming piles as large as a couple of tons of coal, where they would be allowed to rot while the hunters proceeded to refill their wagons with fresh victims . . .'

24 POPULATION SHATTERED

By 1890 the curlew population was shattered. For years the bird has been almost extinct. A few survivors have been spotted but the nest sites are unknown. If conservationists could find those sites they might parlay the last curlews back to strength, but the chances are almost nil.

Hunting would surely have destroyed the whooping crane too but here, at last, the forces of reason and conservation were strong enough to win a little time. The whooper was abundant a century ago. It is a stately creature – some four feet tall with delicate stilt-like legs, an elegant neck, a snow-white body with a dark red face mask and black tips on the seven-foot wing span. Its distinctive trumpet call comes from a trachea five feet long, coiled inside its breastbone.

Such a bird was, of course, an easy and spectacular target for the lusty gun-toters of pioneer days. Early sporting publications carried exultant reports of bagging 'the big white fellows.' The toll was heaviest in the 1890s; after that the birds were nearly gone. Since 1916 it has been illegal to shoot them but at least half of the adult cranes that died between 1939 to 1948 were shot during migration.

'Egging,' the child-like pastime that Victorian adults loved, contributed to the losses. So did settlement; as the Prairie marshlands gave way to wheat fields, the birds retreated into the north. By 1938 only twenty-nine whooping cranes remained on earth and nobody knew where they nested.

Then began a continent-wide search jointly sponsored by the Canadian Wildlife Service, the US Fish and Wildlife Service and the National Audubon Society. Professionals and willing amateurs scanned the skies at migration time and searched almost a million square miles of wilderness.

The break came on 30 June 1954. A forest fire was burning inside Wood Buffalo National Park in northern Alberta. Two forestry men, flying low in a helicopter over the surrounding marsh, spotted two adult whoopers and their chicks. The word flashed around the world. Since then – with their breeding grounds jealously protected – the whooper population has risen to about sixty, including a few birds raised in captivity in a Maryland wildlife research station.

Yet the whooper is still hanging on by a thread. Latterly there have been attempts to mine heavy deposits of fossilized oyster shells, used for road surfacing, off the Texas coast. This would drain the whooper's feeding grounds. Thus, although we protect the nesting sites in Canada the bird could still become extinct.

A visitor to the BC coast, the brown pelican feeds mainly on 'trash' fish for which it dives from a height of ten to thirty feet. The recent incidence of thin-shelled and even shell-less eggs laid by these birds has been attributed by some naturalists to the contamination of its food supply by DDT.

128

Most of the ravages described so far were caused by the gun. Today, thanks to conservation laws, hunters are somewhat less of a menace to birdlife. But man inadvertently kills in other ways.

Thousands of birds die annually by flying full tilt against the lighted windows of city skyscrapers; particularly during migration. Thoughtful companies now dim their lights, at least during those seasons. Recently a specialist with the Canadian Wildlife Service estimated that five million birds die of lead poisoning each year, by swallowing shotgun pellets from lakes and marshes with the gravel they gather for their crops. An estimated 6,000 tons of lead shot are sprayed over North America every year, and five or six ingested pellets will kill a bird. In late 1973 Canada's National Research Council announced it had developed a lead-iron shotgun pellet that would eliminate mortality in at least ninety percent of the birds that ingest it. The next step will be to ban pure lead shot.

Destruction of habitat – sometimes innocently – has destroyed or threatened some species. One such is the greater prairie chicken. Once it ranged over much of Alberta, Saskatchewan and Manitoba, and small parts of Ontario. But when the ploughs turned under the grassland the prairie chicken's home went with it. The booming strutting mating dance of the male chicken at dawn – one of the genuine thrills in nature – is gone from the west.

A few birds lived on Manitoulin Island but interbred with the closely related sharptailed grouse. Now, says Dr Godfrey of the National Museum of Natural Sciences, there may be no pure strain of the greater prairie chicken remaining in Canada.

But the greatest threats to birds today – particularly birds of prey such as our peregrine falcon, bald eagle, osprey, prairie falcon and Richardson's pigeon hawk – is the poison

The breeding range of the Kirtland's warbler is confined to a tiny area of jack pine forest in Michigan. Always an infrequent visitor to Ontario, it is now almost never seen in Canada. A factor in its precarious position seems to be the parasitic habits of the cowbird which lays its eggs in the warbler's nests.

in pesticides and fungicides. These include the chlorinated hydrocarbons such as DDT, dieldrin, aldrin, hepchlor, chlordane, lindane, endrin; a variety of mercury compounds used as seed dressings to inhibit fungus; and the polychlorinate diphenyls used in plastics manufacturing.

With birds the danger is not necessarily direct or immediate death by poison, but a cumulative chain-reaction effect. The use of DDT, a nerve poison, is now sharply restricted in Canada, but DDT is stable. Fifteen years after an application, half of it may still be found in the environment. It can be carried by air or water. It is almost insoluble in water but highly soluble in fats. Thus, DDT and DDE —a similar poison produced from DDT by the chemical processes within living organisms – gathers in the body fat of animals.

25 POTENCY INCREASES

It is particularly harmful to those creatures at the top of the food chain. A frog may eat a DDT-poisoned insect; a fish eats the frog; an eagle or osprey eats the fish. With each step the deadly potency increases.

DDT in sufficient amounts can cause convulsions and tremors in birds. Lesser amounts may cause no visible damage but can interfere with reproduction. A bird's liver seems to produce chemicals directed at the poison but which also break down certain hormones. One of these governs the production of calcium for eggshells. Affected females lay thinshelled eggs which break in the nest, or cause dehydration of the embryo through loss of water. Female ospreys affected by chemicals sometimes lay eggs unusually late in the season, or not at all.

The poisons may also lie dormant in a healthy bird's body, only to become lethal in times of stress. In a US experiment with two groups of quail, non-lethal amounts of DDT were added to the food of one group. Then both were denied food for a short time. All the DDT recipients died. Presumably, during a famine or a harsh winter, when fat stored in a bird's body is utilized as energy, a heavy quota of stored poison is also released into the bloodstream.

Pesticides aren't the only hazard for our birds of prey. They're still being shot as pests. In 1971 hunters in helicopters slaughtered more than 700 federally protected eagles in Wyoming ranch country (the birds were allegedly carrying off lambs). Falcons are increasingly sought, here and abroad, for the once-esoteric sport of falconry which underwent a revival in the 1960s. Stimulated partly by a rash of wildlife films on television, which suggested it was easy and fun to keep a bird of prey, some people who hadn't the know-how to raise a budgie were shackling falcons in their backyards or carrying them, hooded, on their shoulders. Many of the birds died, dirty and neglected. The black market price remains high. Not long ago a Thunder Bay bird lover and keeper of a game sanctuary was given two captured peregrines. She promptly turned them over to the Canadian Wildlife Service in Edmonton, for release in the wilderness – but not before she'd received a surreptitious offer of $40,000 for each bird.

What can we do to save the vanishing birds? The very fact that endangered species are now recognized and reported is an encouragement. Sanctuaries and stiff hunting regulations have brought at least three species back from the brink of extinction: Ross's goose, greater snow goose and trumpeter swan. And the story of the whooping crane, in particular, shows what humans can do if a cause catches their fancy.

The whooping crane case holds out additional hope for other endangered birds. At the Patuxent Wildlife Research Station near Laurel, Maryland, where whoopers are being raised in captivity, it's hoped that some day whooping crane eggs, laid in captivity, can be farmed out to nests of sandhill cranes. If this foster parent plan works, the sandhills would hatch the eggs and raise the young whoopers (the species are closely related).

Other scientists are following similar paths. In 1972 a biology professor at the State University of New York presided over the hatching of two batches of peregrine falcon eggs. The parents were bred in captivity – a rare feat, because their mating ritual includes a soaring flight that is impossible in a cage. The biologist built the falcons a hawk house in his back yard, with sun shelves, padded perches and a ledge that simulated a rock cliff.

The same year, three golden eagle chicks, believed to be the first ever produced by artificial insemination, were hatched at Cornell University. Others are exploring a similar program for the osprey. If more endangered species could be bred in captivity and turned over to foster parents in the wild, we might restore the populations.

Alternatively, it has been suggested that zoos forsake all or part of their traditional role as wildlife showcases, to become wildlife survival centres: breeding and maintaining vanishing species. Most naturalists feel that this would or should be a stopgap measure. What purpose wildlife if not in the wilderness? But this means more parks and sanctuaries are essential and we must earmark the land before it is lost to other uses.

Private non-profit organizations, such as Ducks Unlimited, do a valuable service in helping retain a habitat for the birds. But the onus is primarily on governments, which wield so much power and control so much wealth in today's world. And as the authors of *Last Survivors* note, 'It is seldom easy to convince those in political control of the need to look to the long term advantages inherent in the conservation of wildlife and natural resources, instead of being guided by short term expediency . . .'

Governments move painfully slow. In Canada, only Ontario has an endangered species act, introduced in 1971. It is a valuable act, providing a $3,000 fine and six months in jail for offenders, but it took two years for the first endangered species to be named. But governments *will* act quickly if they deem it politically expedient. It is up to a concerned public to raise an outcry against senseless killing, laws being ignored, precious parkland being lost.

And this in turn comes down to how much we *care*. Is it important to save an obscure species or a dwindling race that, to an average bird watcher, is indistinguishable from

The loggerhead shrike's favourite food is large insects; like all shrikes it sometimes impales them on thorns or barbed wire. It has almost disappeared from Ontario.
Overleaf: *Man's increasing use of the land and water is forcing the common loon to move to more remote habitats.*

132

another race? Is the world poorer without the dodo or the great auk? Does it really matter if the Ispwich sparrow disappears from the earth?

Some naturalists – unable to stir the human conscience in any other way – try to justify birdlife in material terms. White pelicans attract tourists, they point out, and furthermore are indicators of contaminants in our environment which could eventually harm humans. Predators are part of nature's harmony; when we upset the balance by slaughtering a family of hawks, we expose our crops and gardens to hordes of small rodents.

'To maintain sanity in his crowded, polluted artificial world, man may occasionally need to watch a duck braking for a watery landing at dawn,' writes Bob Ingraham, conservation editor of the Canadian Wildlife Federation. 'Not only is our mental health improved by our enjoyment of wildlife, but our physical health benefits from some uses of wildlife.' And he cites examples of how the use of other creatures in laboratory experiments have helped conquer human diseases.

The handsome prairie falcon finds its prey mainly in dry, open grasslands, although it sometimes hunts in wooded and mountainous regions. It breeds in the southern parts of British Columbia, Alberta and Saskatchewan and the species has been sighted on occasion in southern Manitoba. As with many other species, the prairie falcon was once numerous but is now considered by many ornithologists to be in danger of extinction. Hunting and the takeover by man of much of the bird's former breeding range have contributed to its dwindling numbers. The species prefers to nest on rocky ledges protected–as here–with an overhang. This falcon, often confused with the peregrine, is about the size of a crow and decidedly lighter in colour. Like the endangered peregrine falcon, the prairie falcon often lays eggs with faulty shell or with no shell at all. Individual birds and families winter in their breeding range but others fly as far as Mexico on their migratory flights.

26 A MATTER OF CONSCIENCE

But surely there is a deeper rationale, and surely it *does* come down to a matter of conscience. The human race can not forever go on wasting finite resources, and ravaging lesser forms of life. Each species and subspecies is a natural product of a natural world, a miniature work of art. Without it, the world will never again be quite the same. Change is inevitable, but thoughtless destruction is unforgiveable.

In April 1933, the last heath hen – a small bird with a call that 'ended in the air like a Scotch ballad' – died on Martha's Vineyard island, along the New England coast. The editor of the *Vineyard Gazette* wrote, 'When most living things die, they seem only to revert to the central theme of existence from which they were temporarily detached. There is a spirit of vitality everywhere which enfolds the dead with a countenance of consolation and bestows upon the living races more than has been taken away. But to the heath hen, something more than death has happened . . .

'There is no survivor, there is no future, there is no life to be created in this form again. We are looking upon the uttermost finality which can be written, glimpsing the darkness which will not know another ray of life. We are in touch with the reality of extinction.'

This is a responsibility that each of us bears. It is a chilling thought, as we contemplate the fate of the Ipswich sparrow.

ROBERT COLLINS

PART SIX
BIRD WATCHING IN ONE EASY LESSON

The full enjoyment of the vast variety of bird life around us is dependent upon our ability to identify the various species. Identification stimulates the mind and imagination with an endless series of fascinating associations, details, and questions.

It is important to know, for instance, that the light grey jay-sized bird with the white patches set in black wings and tail, which is admired by visitors to our mountain parks, is Clark's nutcracker. It was named after William Clark, co-leader of the famous Lewis and Clark expedition which crossed the continent in 1801-06. A female merganser will actually baby-sit the ducklings of another female who has gone off to feed. And why does the great-crested flycatcher, which builds its nest out of trash, in a cavity, so often choose snakeskin as a material?

When Cartier landed on Funk Island he found it overflowing with gannets (opposite) *and great auks. The auk survived into the nineteenth century when massive assaults exterminated the bird. The Canadian Wildlife Service now restricts visitors.*

Methods of identification have evolved somewhat since the white man's early days in North America, when almost all birds were new and unclassified.

John Burroughs, a late nineteenth century American who did much to popularize nature study, published a book called *Wake Robin* in which he advised: 'First find your bird; observe its ways, its song, its calls, its flight, its haunts, and then shoot it (not ogle it with a glass), and compare with Audubon. In this way the feathered kingdom will soon be conquered.'

Even Thoreau, the naturalist and author of *Walden*, once carried a gun in order to take new or rare birds. Later he decided, as Burroughs did, that he could learn more by paying close attention to the habits of birds and he put his gun aside.

All you need to begin bird watching is a field guide for identification, and binoculars.

A good field guide should be well bound to stand up to constant use, and small enough to slip easily into the pocket of a knapsack or jacket. Make certain you choose a guide that identifies the species in your part of the country.

The guide should include silhouette illustrations of birds, and should specify the identifying marks for each species. It should tell you each bird's preferred nesting habitat, and the extent of its range in summer and winter. It should note any similar species that might confuse identification.

Most field guides contain a few colour plates of selected species. Because lighting is never constant, and because birds are often in molt, these plates seldom approximate the impression you get on seeing the live bird. Do not rely on the colour plates for identification; use the illustrations to reinforce your determination to see new species. Keep a few blank pages in the guide for notes; you will often be too busy trying to get a good view of your bird to flip through the guide at the same time.

Plan to let your guide become marked and dog-eared as necessary. It's not called a field guide without reason. There are other countless books filled with coloured illustrations to grace your library shelves.

You will need a good set of binoculars: two short, parallel telescopes joined together. By presenting each eye with an image, they provide the impression of three dimensional depth and solidity we are used to in unassisted vision. Generally, their excellence depends on the quality of the lenses and how accurately parallel the barrels are.

Most binoculars are designated with two figures (7 x 35, for example) plus a field of view. The initial figure (7) indicates the power of magnification. The second represents the diameter in millimetres of the large lenses at the thicker end of the barrels, and its size determines the amount of light the barrels can collect. As a general rule, for bird watching, the second digit should be at least five times as great as the magnifying power.

The field of view is usually provided in a statement such as 'x' yards at 1,000 yards. This means that at a distance of

After the great auk was extirpated, large colonies of murres inhabited Funk Island. A vigorous attack was mounted on these gentle birds which were carted off by the schooner-ful. Once again, however, Funk Island is vibrant with the cacophony of millions of seabirds.

1,000 yards, you are focussed on a view *x* yards wide. This field narrows as you focus on objects closer to you. Since you will often use your binoculars to watch birds close at hand, you should get the widest field of view possible.

Choose binoculars that are light, and small enough to tuck under your jacket during wet weather. To test a binocular's qualities before you buy, focus on some distant object. Choose an object that has sharply defined vertical and horizontal lines. Get the best focus in the centre of the field. There should be no distortion, vertically or horizontally. The higher the quality of image, the smaller the range of adjustment for sharp focus should be.

Then adjust the binoculars to expand the image toward the edge of the field of view. The image should remain sharp.

If you want binoculars with a magnifying power greater than eight, plan on using a tripod. Most naturalists switch to small telescopes beyond this range.

Prices of binoculars vary between about $20 and nearly $500. My present binoculars cost me $16 about ten years ago. Since then they have been dropped in mud many times, and one eye ring has been knocked off, so that I've taken to using only one barrel, which, I've discovered, is adequate for *my* needs.

Identification involves more than merely noting colour. In many species, it is difficult to distinguish between male and female. The plumage of immature birds can be confusing. The immature bald eagle, which has a dusky head, is frequently mistaken for the mature golden eagle. The male rose-breasted grosbeak loses his stunning red breast patch entirely during molt. The male indigo bunting turns brown. The only reliable markings of the black-bellied plover in fall are black wingpits and a whitish rump and tail.

Identification therefore becomes a matter of putting together many shreds of evidence. Did it have a roller-coaster

Fortunate indeed would be the bird watcher who spotted even one whooping crane. The large and impressive bird is surviving by a thin thread: there are only about sixty birds remaining in the world. Recent vigorous attempts to protect and encourage the whooper show promise of hope for this spectacular bird.

142

Back from the brink

The whooping crane once ranged over southwestern North America, breeding in flat, marshy country. However the large, showy crane was an easy and apparently irresistable target for gun hunters, and by 1916, when shooting the whooper finally became illegal, it was nearly finished. The spread of agriculture over its breeding range has contributed to the bird's decline, but even after the law forbidding hunting was passed, many birds lost thereafter were shot during migration. The whooper is now known to breed only in Wood Buffalo Park, southern Mackenzie and it winters at the Aransas Wildlife Refuge on the Texas coast. Though long-lived it breeds just once a year and normally lays only two eggs, thus its reproductive potential is limited. A gregarious bird, the whooping crane's exuberant behaviour is thrilling to watch, should one happen to be in the right southern Saskatchewan grainfield at the right migratory moment. Their lively antics may often be associated with mating rituals but they don't seem to be restricted to this purpose. Even the young cranes will sometimes perform a spirited 'dance,' leaping into the air, bowing and stretching, tossing about bits of twigs and grass. These cranes were photographed in Saskatchewan during a stopover in their long and dangerous migration.

145

Two flourishing species

Not all birds are on a downhill population spiral. Many species have been introduced, or have introduced themselves, into new habitats which have proved extremely hospitable. Some birds have become only too successful in adapting to these new conditions – we are now overrun by the house sparrow and the starling. The white cattle egret (opposite) *is a bird that is increasing its range. The first one was spotted in the new world about ninety years ago in Surinam, and there is evidence that it had spread to North America by around 1940. Since then it has steadily moved north and has been breeding in eastern Canada since 1962. A bird watcher recently spotted the first cattle egret in the Northwest Territories. This small white heron is a frequent companion of grazing cattle which stir up clouds of insects, the bird's favourite food.* Above: *The trumpeter swan was once severely threatened by hunting and the usurption of a large part of its breeding range. However, conservation efforts have been successful and this large, elegant bird is now considered out of danger. It is being reintroduced in Swan Lake, British Columbia. It is not at all unusual for foreign species to find a suitable habitat in a new land; the cardinal first arrived in Canada from the tropics around the turn of the century.*

146

flight, or did it fly flat out? Did it have a crest or top knot? Was the tail forked? Rounded? Square tipped? What was its habitat? The edge of a meadow? A marsh? Could the bird be a migrant?

The ability to aurally identify birds in the field is important. Roger Tory Peterson estimates that experts do ninety percent of their identification by sound. You can learn to recognize many birds by listening carefully to recordings of bird songs.

Consider joining the nature study group in your community. These organizations hold meetings, publish newsletters, and conduct outings throughout most of the year, and they welcome new members. Their hikes are usually easy affairs; the intention is to see birds, not to set up endurance tests, so don't hold back from participating. You will quickly discover the best local bird-watching areas, and all those extra eyes and ears will introduce you to many birds you would otherwise not likely spot.

A word about 'bird golf.' You may be drawn into the game. Bird golf is an informal competition which involves correctly identifying species and comparing counts. Unlike the other golf, the highest score wins. The competition may span a day, a week, or a lifetime. It can be played over long distances, or, like solitaire, against oneself. The on-going part of the game pits 'life list,' which is the sum total of species identified over a lifetime, against your 'opponent's' life list.

You may enjoy bird golf; personally, I abhor it. I've seen bird golfers tramping along, calling out 'phoebe to the left' or 'kinglets overhead' without breaking stride. I cannot understand it. I want to see the bird. The closer, the better. I've never glimpsed either species of the kinglet at close quarters. Does the ruby-crowned kinglet really expose his crown in a state of excitement? I'd wait all day for the opportunity to see for myself.

Your 'style' of bird watching in the field will depend a great deal on your physical condition, the habitat you are exploring, and the time of year. Early morning tends to be the birds' most active period of the day. Activity tapers off toward midday and is somewhat renewed in the evening.

I have a friend whose technique is to move along as rapidly and as silently as possible. His goal is to surprise birds, and get close to them before they fly away.

I read once about a man who liked watching hawks. He learned that hawks will avoid an upright human figure, but that they become curious when the figure is still and stretched out upon the ground. Eventually a raptor would discover him and approach. I've tried this method a few times, but a Tom Sawyer itch or impatience to look around at what else is going on always prompts me, I suspect, to get up and move along too soon.

I prefer sitting quietly, usually with my back up against a trunk or a bank so that I'm hidden from behind. It's not so necessary to be still and quiet as it is to feel relaxed and at one with your surroundings. Birds, I'm convinced, can often sense when they are not threatened. The first time I tried this approach, a pileated woodpecker landed on the side of a stump about five feet in front of me. This technique works particularly well early in the season when the pressures of mating, nest building, and rearing young are greatest.

One of the more sophisticated methods of enticing wild birds into view uses tape-recorded bird songs. Most of the songs available on record albums are now available also on cassettes and reels. On hearing a certain species, you play the corresponding song on your portable machine, and the individual bird whose territory you've invaded will usually fly into sight in search of the 'interloper.'

Many wild birds can be attracted to your garden by providing bird houses, or by creating ideal nesting sites. Provincial wildlife branches publish excellent booklets on this subject; so does the Canadian Wildlife Service in Ottawa. Follow the instructions closely, for the dimensions have been arrived at after many years of trial and observation. The entrance for the bluebird, for instance, should be no greater than one-and-one-half inches in order to keep starlings out.

Until 1962 the little gull appeared to be only a casual and rare visitor to the western hemisphere. Since then, however, when a few were found nesting in Ontario, they have been breeding in small numbers in the Great Lakes region and the Atlantic coast and have been occasionally sighted in Saskatchewan.

Different species like different foods. Robins, catbirds, and thrushes will take seedless raisins and cooking currants. So will grosbeaks. Hummingbirds are easily attracted to small glass feeders containing sugared water and red vegetable colouring. In winter months, hang suet from tree limbs. Seed for the seed eaters – usually a mixture of millet, rape, hemp, flax, sunflower, and corn – can usually be purchased from local millers who will likely know the mix most suitable for the species in your area.

Many wild birds can be tamed to take food from your hands. If you have a shelf feeder beside a window, you can accustom the birds to your presence by leaving the arm of an old jacket in the window, with a stuffed glove at the end. Cover the palm of the stuffed glove with seed. As the birds gain confidence they will perch on the glove to feed. When you feel they are ready to accept hand feeding, put your hand through the sleeve. Wear the glove on your hand the first few times. Eventually, with patience, you will be feeding with your bare hand.

An upright dummy in the garden can be used in the same manner. Spread the food across the dummy's outstretched arms and across its shoulders, then take the dummy's place whenever you wish.

Hand feeding wild birds takes patience and a calm approach. Different species exhibit different degrees of shyness. Try to put yourself in the bird's place. For example, don't swallow when a bird is trying to make up its mind to approach you.

Birds use water for drinking and bathing. An ideal watering place should be made of concrete; its rough surface is easy for tiny feet to grasp. Depth should range from one-half to two inches for small and larger species. A steady drip on the surface seems to most effectively signal the presence of water. The site should be in an open area where predators cannot approach without revealing themselves. There should be nearby trees and shrubs the bird can fly to if it is threatened by a predator.

If you have a cat, forget about attracting wild birds. Even if your pet is rather mangy and decrepit, its presence will tend to disturb birds that might want to feed or nest nearby, in the same way that the sight of a grizzly might unsettle you and make you more wary on a mountain hike.

Provincial authorities often subsidize planting projects or pond construction designed to make estates, recreational acreages, and farms more attractive to birds. Clearings can be cut in woodlots to help food-bearing shrubs to grow. Dead trees left standing are feeding sites for woodpeckers; the cavities they create become nesting holes for other species. Fences that are also hedgerows provide windbreaks, cover, food, and nesting places. Brush piles provide shelter for emergencies and for nesting.

As your familiarity with birds grows, you may find yourself concentrating more and more on some specific activity. You may choose to keep records on nesting successes, territories, feeding habits, departures and arrivals during migration. You may become a bird bander, or participate in projects with your local naturalist society.

Bird photography may interest you. The increasing popularity of this hobby has been helped enormously by the small, light, easy-to-operate 35 mm camera, and by the refined state of colour film processing. Certain accessories, particularly telescopic lenses and a flash attachment, may be necessary.

If you take up bird photography, be prepared to deal with a question of conscience. The most reliable place to photograph birds is at the nesting site. Bird photographers, in their zeal to get in close and to get light on the subject matter, often prevent nesting successes.

Perhaps the time has come for bird photographers to stay away from nests, just as Burroughs and Thoreau once put their guns aside. Challenge yourself to discover other ways to take exciting photographs. Place a feeder in a window with lots of light; photograph from inside when a bird alights to feed. Drape the twigs of trees with suet, and as winter visitors nibble at it, take your picture. If you *must* photograph a nesting bird, build a blind at some distance from the nest and use a telescopic lens.

WAYNE McLAREN

BIBLIOGRAPHY

BOOKS

ALEXANDER, W.B., *Birds of the Ocean*, New York: Putnam, 1954

AMADON, DEAN, "Some Consideration of Bird Migration," *Science*, Vol. 108, 1948

AMERICAN ORNITHOLOGISTS' UNION, *Checklist of North American Birds*, New York: AOU, 1957

AMOS, WILLIAM H., *The Life of the Seashore*, Toronto: McGraw-Hill, 1966

AUDUBON, J.J., *The Birds of America*, New York: 1840

BENT, A.C., *Life Histories of North American Warblers*, New York: Dover Publications Inc., 1963

BODSWORTH, FRED, *Last of the Curlews*, New York: Dodd Mead & Co., 1954

BROOKS, A. and H.S. SWARTH, *A Distributional List of the Birds of British Columbia*, Berkeley: Cooper Club, 1925

CHAPMAN, F.M., *The Warblers of North America*, New York: Dover Publications Inc, 1968

DAVIDSON, A.R., *Annotated List of the Birds of Southern Vancouver Island*, Victoria: Victoria Natural History Society, 1966

DORST, JEAN, *The Migration of Birds*, Boston: Houghton Mifflin, 1963

DRENT, R.H. and C.J. GUIGUET, *A Catalogue of British Columbia Sea-bird Colonies*, Victoria: Provincial Museum, Occasional Papers No. 12, 1961

EDWARDS, R.Y. and R.W. RITCEY *The Birds of Wells Gray Park*, Victoria: Parks Branch, 1967

FISHER, JAMES and DANA E. WALLACE, *Sea-Birds*, Boston: Houghton Mifflin, 1954

GABRIELSON, I.N. and F.C. LINCOLN, *Birds of Alaska*, Washington: Wildlife Management Institute, 1959

GODFREY, W. EARL, *Birds of the Cypress Hills and Flotten Lake Regions, Saskatchewan*, Ottawa, National Museum of Canada, Bulletin 120, 1950

GODFREY, W. EARL, *The Birds of Canada*, Ottawa, National Museum of Canada, 1966

GRIEVE, SYMINGTON, *The Great Auk or Garefowl*, London: 1885

GRIFFIN, D.R., *Bird Migration*, Garden City: Doubleday, 1964

GRISCOM, L. and A. SPRUNT JR (eds), *The Warblers of North America*, New York: Gavin-Adair, 1957

GUIGUET, C.J., *The Birds of British Columbia: Owls*, Victoria: Provincial Museum, 1960

GUIGUET, C.J., *The Birds of British Columbia: Upland Game Birds*, Victoria, Provincial Museum, 1955

GUIGUET C.J., *The Birds of British Columbia: Waterfowl*, Victoria: Provincial Museum, 1958

HOFFMAN, R., *Birds of the Pacific States*, Boston: Houghton Mifflin, 1927

HORN, E.O., 'Birds of the Arctic,' *The Beaver*, Winnipeg: Hudson's Bay Company, Summer 1959

IRVING, L. and J. KROG, 'Body Temperature of Arctic and Subarctic Birds and Mammals,' *Journal of Applied Physics*, Vol. 6, 1954

JAQUES, H.E. and R. OLLIVIER, *How to Know the Water Birds*, Dubuque: W.C. Brown Co, 1960

JEWETT, S.A., W.P. TAYLOR, W.T. SHAW and J.W. ALDRICH, *Birds of Washington State*, Seattle: University of Washington Press, 1953

JOHNSTONE, W.B., *The Birds of the East Kootenay, British Columbia*, Victoria: Provincial Museum, 1949

KEITH, L.B., *Wildlife's Ten-year Cycle*, Madison: University of Wisconsin Press, 1963

KENDIEGH, S. CHARLES, *Bird Population Studies in the Coniferous Forest Biome during a Spruce Budworm Outbreak*, Toronto: Ontario Department of Lands and Forests, Biological Bulletin No. 1, 1947

KORTRIGHT, F.H., *The Ducks, Geese and Swans of North America*, Washington: American Wildlife Institute, 1942

LANYON, WESLEY E., *Biology of Birds*, New York: Natural History Press, 1963

LINDUSKA, J.P., (ed), *Waterfowl Tomorrow*, Washington: US Department of the Interior, Bureau of Sports, Fisheries and Wildlife, 1964

LIVINGSTON, JOHN A., (Illustrated by J. Fenwick Lansdowne), *Birds of the Eastern Forest* (two volumes), Toronto: McClelland and Stewart, 1968, 1970

LIVINGSTON, JOHN A., (Illustrated by J. Fenwick Lansdowne), *Birds of the Northern Forest*, Toronto: McClelland and Stewart, 1966

LOCKLEY, R.M., *Puffins*, New York: Doubleday, 1962

MITCHELL, MARGARET H., *The Passenger Pigeon in Ontario*, Toronto: University of Toronto Press/Royal Ontario Museum 1935

MUNRO, J.A., *Observations of Birds and Mammals in Central British Columbia*, Victoria: Provincial Museum, 1950

MUNRO, J.A. and I. MCT. COWAN, *Review of the Bird Fauna of British Columbia*, Victoria: Provincial Museum, 1947

MYRES, M.T., *The European Starling in British Columbia*, Victoria: Provincial Museum, Occasional Papers No. 11, 1958

NOVAKOWSKI, N.S., *Whooping Crane Population Dynamics*, Ottawa: Canadian Wildlife Service, Report Series No. 1, Department of Indian Affairs and Northern Development, 1966

PETERS, HAROLD S. and T.D. BURLEIGH, *Birds of Newfoundland*, St John's: Department of Natural Resources, 1951

PETERS, STUART S., 'Food Habits of the Newfoundland Willow Ptarmigan,' *Journal of Wildlife Management*, Vol. 22, No. 4, 1958

PETERSON, ROGER TORY, *A Field Guide to the Birds*, Boston: Houghton Mifflin, 1947

PETERSON, ROGER TORY, *A Field Guide to Western Birds*, Boston: Houghton Mifflin, 1941

PETERSON, ROGER TORY and THE EDITORS OF LIFE, *The Birds*, New York: Time-Life Books, 1965

PETTINGILL, O.S. JR, *Ornithology*, Minneapolis: Burgess Publishing Co, 1969

PETTINGILL, O.S. JR (ed), *The Bird Watcher's America*, New York: McGraw-Hill, 1965

PITELKA, FRANK A., 'Distribution of Birds in Relation to Major Biotic Communities,' *American Midland Naturalist*, Vol. 25, 1941

POUGH, RICHARD H., *Audubon Land Bird Guide*, Garden City: Doubleday, 1946

POUGH, RICHARD H., *Audubon Water Bird Guide*, Garden City: Doubleday, 1951

POUGH, RICHARD H., *Audubon Western Bird Guide*, Garden City: Doubleday, 1957

ROBBINS, C.S., BERTEL BRUUN, and HERBERT Z. ZIM, (Illustrated by Arthur Singer), *A Fieldguide to the Birds of North America*, New York: Golden Press, 1966

SALT, W.R. and A.L. WILK, *The Birds of Alberta*, Edmonton: Queen's Printer, 1966

SCHOLANDER, P.F., R. HOCK, U. WALTERS and L. IRVING, *Adaptations to Cold in Arctic and Tropical Mammals and Birds in Relation to Body Temperature, Insulation and Basal Metabolic Rate*, Ottawa: Biological Bulletin No. 99, pps 259-271

SNYDER, L.L., *Arctic Birds of Canada*, Toronto: University of Toronto Press, 1957

SNYDER, L.L. and T.M. SHORTT, *Ontario Birds*, Toronto: Clarke Irwin & Co, 1951

SPEIRS, J. MURRAY, 'Birds of Ontario's Coniferous Forest Region,' *Canadian Audubon*, Vol. 31, No. 2, Mar - Apr 1969

SQUIRES, W.A., *The Birds of New Brunswick*, St John: New Brunswick Museum, 1952

STIRRET, GEORGE M., *Spring Birds of Point Pelee National Park*, Ottawa: Department of Northern Affairs and National Resources, 1960

TAVERNER, P.A., *Birds of Western Canada*, Ottawa: National Museum of Canada, 1923

TUFTS, ROBIE W., *The Birds of Nova Scotia*, Halifax: Nova Scotia Museum, 1961

VAN TYNE, JOSSELYN, and ANDREW J. BERGER, *The Fundamentals of Ornithology*, New York and London: John Wylie & Sons, 1959

VERMEER, KEES, *The Breeding Ecology of the Glaucous-winged Gull*, Victoria: Provincial Museum, Occasional Papers No. 13, 1963

WETMORE, ALEXANDER and others, *Birds and Creatures*, Washington: the Smithsonian Institution, 1936

PERIODICALS

Canadian Audubon, Toronto: Canadian Audubon Society

Canadian Field Naturalist, Ottawa: Ottawa Field Naturalists' Club

Condor, Berkeley: Cooper Ornithological Society, Museum of Vertebrate Zoology

Murrelet, Seattle: Pacific Northwest Bird and Mammal Society, Washington State Museum

Ontario Naturalist, Toronto: Federation of Ontario Naturalists

INDEX

Page numbers in italics refer to illustrations.

ACKNOWLEDGEMENTS AND CREDITS

The authors and editors of this volume wish to thank the following organizations and individuals whose assistance with the text and illustrations made this book possible: Fred Bodsworth, Toronto; Bill Brooks, Toronto; Canadian Wildlife Service, Ottawa; Dr F. G. Cooch, Canadian Wildlife Service, Ottawa; Dr Fred Cooke, Department of Biology, Queen's University, Kingston, Ontario; Dr Donald R. Gunn, Toronto; Dr Brian K. Hall, Department of Biology, Dalhousie University, Halifax, Nova Scotia; Dr Ross James, Department of Ornithology, Royal Ontario Museum, Toronto; Dr R. A. Liversage, Department of Zoology, University of Toronto; Dr David McCallion, Department of Anatomy, McMaster University, Hamilton, Ontario; Dr C. McGowan, Department of Vertebrate Paleontology, Royal Ontario Museum, Toronto; Gerald McKeating, Federation of Ontario Naturalists, Toronto; Dr John Ostrom, Department of Paleontology, Peabody Museum, Yale University, New Haven, Connecticut, USA; Judith Parsons, Federation of Ontario Naturalists, Toronto; Dr George K. Peck, Oakville, Ontario; Barry Ranford, Toronto; Kaari Turk, Toronto; Brian Tyson, Toronto; and Joanne Vano, Audio-Visual Department, Ontario Science Centre, Toronto.

Where more than one picture appears on a page, the order of credits is left to right, horizontal separated by commas, vertical separated by semi-colons.

Cover	Robert Bateman
Back Cover	James and Carmichael
1	Barry Ranford
2	Robert Bateman
4	Barry Ranford
6	Barry Ranford
9	Bill Brooks
10	Huntley Brown
12	Norman R. Lightfoot, Barbara K. Deans; Barry Ranford, Norman R. Lightfoot; James and Carmichael, Barry Ranford
13,14	Barry Ranford
16	Huntley Brown
19	Dr George K. Peck
20	Norman R. Lightfoot, Dr George K. Peck, T. W. Hall, T. W. Hall; Barbara K. Deans, Barry Ranford, Dr George K. Peck, Dr George K. Peck; Norman R. Lightfoot, Barry Ranford,

	Dr Donald R. Gunn, T. W. Hall	76,78	Barry Ranford
21	Barbara K. Deans, W. D. Woods; T. W. Hall, T. W. Hall; Ted Maginn, Dr Donald R. Gunn	80	Barbara K. Deans
22	Huntley Brown	82	Norman R. Lightfoot
24	Michael Foster	84,85	Barry Ranford
25,27	T. W. Hall	86,87	James and Carmichael
28	Robert Bateman	88	Robert Bateman
30	Norman R. Lightfoot	90	James and Carmichael
31,32	T. W. Hall	92,94	Barry Ranford
36	Huntley Brown	95,96	James and Carmichael
38, 39	Vlasta van Kampen	97,98	Barry Ranford
40,41	Barry Ranford	100	Dr Donald R. Gunn
42,45	Dr Donald R. Gunn	101	Huntley Brown
46	Robert Bateman	102	Robert Taylor
50	Ted Maginn	104	Robert Bateman
52	Vlasta van Kampen	107,108	Barry Ranford
53	C. G. Hampson	111,112	Barry Ranford
54	James M. Richards, Janet Green, James M. Richards; Dr George K. Peck, James M. Richards, Dr George K. Peck	113	Barbara K. Deans
		114,115	Barry Ranford
		116	C. G. Hampson
		117,119	Barry Ranford
55	Barry Ranford, James M. Richards, Barry Ranford; James and Carmichael, James M. Richards, Barry Ranford	120	Vlasta van Kampen
		122,124	T. W. Hall
		125	Bill Brooks
56	Huntley Brown	126,129	Dr George K. Peck
57	Dr George K. Peck, Barry Ranford, Barry Ranford, Barry Ranford; Dr George K. Peck, Barry Ranford, Dr George K. Peck, Barry Ranford; James M. Richards, Barry Ranford, Robert Taylor, Barry Ranford; Barry Ranford, James M. Richards, James M. Richards, Barry Ranford	130	Dr George K. Peck
		133	Barry Ranford
		134	Robert Bateman
		136	C. G. Hampson
		138	Barbara K. Deans
		140	Barry Ranford
		142,144	Fred W. Lahrman
		145	Fred W. Lahrman
58,59	Dr Brian K. Hall	146	Bill Brooks, James and Carmichael
60	Dr George K. Peck	149	James and Carmichael
63	James and Carmichael		
64	Barry Ranford		
66	James and Carmichael		
68	Barry Ranford		
70	Barbara K. Deans		
72	Mildred McPhee		
74,75	Barry Ranford		
77	Vlasta van Kampen		

This book was produced entirely in Canada by: Mono Lino Typesetting Co. Limited/*Typesetting;* Herzig Somerville Limited/*Film Separation;* Ashton-Potter Limited/*Printing;* T. H. Best Printing Co. Limited/*Binding. Typefaces: Times New Roman and Helvetica. Paper: 64 lb. Georgian Offset Smooth.*